VIETNAM STUDIES

THE ROLE OF
MILITARY INTELLIGENCE
1965-1967

by

Major General Joseph A. McChristian

DEPARTMENT OF THE ARMY
WASHINGTON, D.C., 1974

Library of Congress Catalog Card Number: 74–600003

First Printing

For sale by the Superintendent of Documents, U.S. Government Printing Office
Washington, D.C. 20402 - Price $2.45
Stock Number 0820–00499

Foreword

The United States Army has met an unusually complex challenge in Southeast Asia. In conjunction with the other services, the Army has fought in support of a national policy of assisting an emerging nation to develop governmental processes of its own choosing, free of outside coercion. In addition to the usual problems of waging armed conflict, the assignment in Southeast Asia has required superimposing the immensely sophisticated tasks of a modern army upon an underdeveloped environment and adapting them to demands covering a wide spectrum. These involved helping to fulfill the basic needs of an agrarian population, dealing with the frustrations of antiguerrilla operations, and conducting conventional campaigns against well-trained and determined regular units.

It is still necessary for the Army to continue to prepare for other challenges that may lie ahead. While cognizant that history never repeats itself exactly and that no army ever profited from trying to meet a new challenge in terms of the old one, the Army nevertheless stands to benefit immensely from a study of its experience, its shortcomings no less than its achievements.

Aware that some years must elapse before the official histories will provide a detailed and objective analysis of the experience in Southeast Asia, we have sought a forum whereby some of the more salient aspects of that experience can be made available now. At the request of the Chief of Staff, a representative group of senior officers who served in important posts in Vietnam and who still carry a heavy burden of day-to-day responsibilities has prepared a series of monographs. These studies should be of great value in helping the Army develop future operational concepts while at the same time contributing to the historical record and providing the American public with an interim report on the performance of men and officers who have responded, as others have through our history, to exacting and trying demands.

The reader should be reminded that most of the writing was accomplished while the war in Vietnam was at its peak, and the monographs frequently refer to events of the past as if they were taking place in the present.

All monographs in the series are based primarily on official records, with additional material from published and unpublished secondary works, from debriefing reports and interviews with key participants, and from the personal experience of the author. To facilitate security clearance, annotation and detailed bibliography have been omitted from the published version; a fully documented account with bibliography is filed with the U.S. Army Center of Military History.

Major General Joseph A. McChristian is particularly well qualified to write of the role of military intelligence in Vietnam from 1965 through 1967. During that period he served on the staff of General William C. Westmoreland as Assistant Chief of Staff for Intelligence, U.S. Military Assistance Command, Vietnam.

General McChristian's background in military intelligence is one of long and distinguished service. After World War II he served as Third U.S. Army Assistant Chief of Staff for Intelligence under General George S. Patton, as Third Army Deputy G–2, and as Deputy Director of Intelligence, U.S. Forces, Austria. In 1948 he was assigned to the Intelligence Division of the Department of the Army General Staff. In 1949, during the Greek-Communist War, General McChristian became a member of the first Joint U.S. Military Advisory Group in Athens and, later, from June 1956 through May 1960, he served as U.S. Army Attache to Greece. From January 1962 through February 1963 General McChristian was assigned to the Office of the Assistant Chief of Staff for Intelligence, Department of the Army, where he was Chief of the Western Division of Foreign Intelligence. From April 1963 through June 1965 he served as U.S. Army, Pacific, Assistant Chief of Staff for Intelligence at Fort Shafter, Hawaii; from there he went to Vietnam. In August 1968 he became Chief of Army Intelligence. General McChristian retired from active duty in 1971.

Washington, D.C.   VERNE L. BOWERS
15 December 1973   Major General, USA
                                                                      The Adjutant General

Preface

As General Westmoreland's intelligence officer from 13 July 1965 until 1 June 1967, I am happy to report on the role and development of military intelligence in the Republic of Vietnam during that period. I do so with respect and admiration for the Vietnamese, Koreans, Australians, and Americans who made up that great intelligence team.

Many members of that team assisted me in the preparation of this account. I know they, as I, feel a warm sense of satisfaction in passing on to you some of the knowledge we gained.

The story that follows is mine. I am solely responsible for its content. It is not a complete history; such an undertaking is beyond the purpose and scope of this monograph. My purpose is to record the development and the role of intelligence in Vietnam, not only for students of intelligence but also for planners and decision makers who depend upon intelligence in order to arrive at sound decisions. I have limited the scope of my account to a discussion of some of the major intelligence activities developed in support of the mission of U.S. Military Assistance Command, Vietnam, with consideration of why and how we developed what we did plus lessons learned along the way.

First, I will identify the challenge. Second, I will address developing the organization. Third, I will discuss United States–South Vietnamese combined military intelligence activities. And then, in turn, I will cover intelligence operations, intelligence production, counterintelligence, and intelligence support activities. My last chapter will summarize lessons we learned.

The task of writing this monograph was greatly facilitated by the following dedicated professionals who served with me in Vietnam and who subsequently provided input, suggestions, and advice in its preparation. I thank them for their invaluable assistance and loyalty, and I remember each with admiration and respect: Colonel Frank L. Scofield, U.S. Air Force; Colonel William H. Crosson, U.S. Army; Colonel Robert E. McMahon, U.S. Army; Colonel Glenn E. Muggelberg, U.S. Army; Colonel John T. Little, U.S. Army; Colonel Robert F. Robens, U.S. Army; Colonel John J. Morgan, U.S. Army; Colonel Frank L. Schaf, Jr., U.S. Army; Colonel Robert Churley, U.S. Marine Corps; Colonel Ralph T. Hunt, U.S. Army; Colonel Jerry Dismuke, U.S. Air Force; Colonel C. M. Smith, U.S. Air Force; Colonel Donald T. Ketcham, U.S. Army; Colonel Stone W. Quillian, U.S. Marine Corps; Colonel

Gains B. Hawkins, U.S. Army; Colonel Ralph H. Groover, Jr., U.S. Army; Colonel Walter R. Pierce, Jr., U.S. Army; Colonel Silas E. Chumley, U.S. Army; Colonel Coleman Noahson, U.S. Army; Lieutenant Colonel Autmer Ackley, Jr., U.S. Army; Major James D. Strachan, U.S. Army; Major James E. Crouch, U.S. Army; Sergeant Major Vince LeBlanc, U.S. Army; Master Sergeant Clyde F. Jepson, who, serving as my enlisted aide, conscientiously and loyally saw to it that in all matters relating to subsistence, quarters, health, sanitation, uniforms, and equipment I never had a worry; Colonel Gains B. Hawkins and Lieutenant Colonel Lyle K. Alexander for their assistance in assembling information and drafting this report; and Mrs. Helen Worden for her cheerful help in editing and typing my final draft

Washington, D.C.   JOSEPH A. McCHRISTIAN
15 December 1973   Major General, U.S. Army, Retired

Contents

Charts

Illustrations

THE ROLE OF MILITARY
INTELLIGENCE

CHAPTER I

Introduction

The Challenge

"Find the enemy!" With these words General Harold K. Johnson, then chief of the staff of the Army, wished me well as I left Washington to become General William C. Westmoreland's assistant chief of staff for intelligence in the Republic of Vietnam. Combat intelligence was not new to me. I knew that finding the enemy was only part of the challenge. Our soldiers would have to fix and fight him. They would need to know enemy strength, capabilities, and vulnerabilities as well as information on the weather and terrain. Such intelligence had to be timely, accurate, adequate, and usable. It was to be my job to build an organization to meet that challenge.

After a series of briefings in Washington and goodbyes in Fort Shafter, Hawaii, I was on my way to serve my country in a third war, albeit in an advisory role, or so I thought. I had just completed two years as Assistant Chief of Staff for Intelligence, U.S. Army, Pacific. During those two years I had traveled from Singapore to Korea visiting United States and allied intelligence activities, including those in South Vietnam. On my last visit there I had presented a study to General Westmoreland and his intelligence staff on my concept for the Army intelligence organization. From Saigon I had gone to Bangkok and presented a similar briefing. I was familiar with the situation in Southeast Asia. I knew that the Viet Cong had better intelligence than we; however, I knew there was much more information available to us if we had the resources and organization to acquire it. The counterinsurgency in Vietnam had unusual intelligence potential in that many enemy military and political organizations were relatively stationary and had assigned areas of operations. We could focus our intelligence efforts on those areas if we knew their locations. During my flight from Honolulu to Saigon I wrote two questions in my notebook: "Where can I normally expect to find the enemy?" and "Where can I normally not expect to find the enemy?" During that flight I wrote scores of answers to each question—every possibility that occurred to me. Later in Saigon we were to refine and reduce the answers to a few elements on which timely and adequate information was available. This became the basis for the pattern analysis technique methodology which permitted us to identify and locate enemy base areas. Consequently, we could focus most of our collection efforts on about 20 percent of the country. This step was important in achieving economy of intelligence effort.

I arrived in Saigon on 29 June 1965. My first days in South Vietnam were spent visiting the field and attending briefings. Major General Carl Youngdale, U.S. Marine Corps, was the Assistant Chief of Staff for Intelligence, J–2, U.S. Military Assistance Command, Vietnam (MACV). We were scheduled to have an overlap of about two weeks. On 13 July, the day that Lieutenant General Carroll, director of the Defense Intelligence Agency, arrived in Saigon, orders were issued assigning me as J–2. While I was waiting at the airport for General Carroll's plane to arrive, a messenger from MACV headquarters informed me that the Secretary of Defense, Mr. Robert S. McNamara, was to arrive on 16 July. I was scheduled to present the lead-off briefing on intelligence. Upon returning to MACV headquarters with General Carroll I learned that Mr. McNamara wanted to know what resources we needed, not as advisers but to help fight the war. I had been the J–2 for only a few hours as an adviser. Now we were at war. We had much to do in a short time. The challenge before me was taking shape—to develop and supervise a U.S. Military Assistance Command, Vietnam, combat intelligence organization.

During the period between my assignment as J–2 and the arrival of Mr. McNamara in Saigon, my staff and I prepared an intelligence briefing and together with the Air Force and Navy staffs developed a list of intelligence units and resources required to support the new combat mission of the MACV commander. Colonel William H. Crosson, the chief of intelligence production, told me that he could not write a valid estimate of enemy capabilities and vulnerabilities because available intelligence was neither timely nor adequate and we were unable to evaluate much of it for accuracy. However, he could write a situation report, and did. The contents of that briefing turned out to be unimportant. Mr. McNamara was interested in learning what we needed in order to do our new job. As I started the briefing he quickly interrupted and asked my views on what was needed to improve intelligence. As a result of that hour-long discussion he asked that a detailed plan be provided to him the next day on my proposals to improve interrogation activities. The briefing pointed up the need for evaluating information, for separating fact from fiction. It further clarified the challenge: we did not have the means.

While part of my staff prepared the briefing, I worked with others to develop for Mr. McNamara a "shopping list" of intelligence resources required. I learned early that we were starting our planning from scratch. No plans or planning guidance concerning the transition from an advisory organization to a combat organization existed within the J–2 staff. From the Operations Directorate, J–3, staff I learned that they

MAJOR GENERAL
JOSEPH A. McCHRISTIAN

had done some planning. They had a computer run of a list of troops under consideration. I asked that a listing of all intelligence units and intelligence-related units be extracted; however, the existing computer programming could not do so. The officer in charge of this activity was not knowledgeable concerning intelligence units except for detachments assigned to divisions. It was apparent that the force structure under consideration did not provide adequately for intelligence. This experience revealed the need for computer programs to be designed to extract intelligence and intelligence-related data and for the intelligence staff to participate in force structure planning. No plans were available to J–2. The challenge continued to grow.

For the next several days we received necessary guidance. My staff and I developed the organization and resources that would be required to support our combat mission. That mission was clear: we were to help the South Vietnamese fight a war to defend themselves and at the same time help them to build a nation.

In order for the MACV commander to have adequate intelligence to conduct a defense of South Vietnam we had to consider a geographical area of intelligence interest much larger than that country itself. Not only must we concern ourselves with intelligence on the military, paramilitary, logistical, and political organizations of the enemy within South Vietnam, but we also had to concern ourselves with the location of enemy forces, logistical supplies, base areas, sanctuaries, trails, roads, and rivers located within Cambodia and Laos as well as throughout North Vietnam. We had to concern ourselves with the air space extending miles beyond the borders of South Vietnam in order to prevent surprise air attack. We were concerned with patrolling the South China Sea bordering South Vietnam and the extensive waterways within the Mekong Delta which were avenues of approach for logistical support and reinforcements for the enemy. Our future organization and requests for resources had to take into consideration our need to collect, evaluate, and produce intelligence on all of those areas. We needed to know the quantity and quality of war materials being supplied by China and the Soviet Union and her satellites. We needed to be kept informed of any changes of Chinese military forces which could influence the war in South Vietnam. Above all, we needed to know the quantity and quality of manpower the enemy could send to South Vietnam and the will of North Vietnamese leaders and soldiers to persist.

It was apparent to me that a large and sophisticated organization would be required. I fully expected that the United States would be involved in combat and later in military assistance for many years. I was convinced that our military assistance would be required until security permitted political stability. I knew from my experiences in the Greek Communist War and my later service there as the military attache, as well as from our experiences in Korea, that many years would pass before South Vietnam could defend itself. It takes a long time to identify and eliminate insurgents. The challenge was clear, the opportunity to demonstrate our professionalism at hand. Now was the time to apply the principles we had learned.

Intelligence Philosophy

Sound decisions depend upon timely, accurate, adequate, and usable information. Wartime decisions carry great responsibility; they affect not only the lives of our fighting men but also the liberty of our people. Decision makers ask questions for which they need answers. In the military, such questions are referred to as essential elements of information (EEI). The number of such important questions should be kept to a minimum. Actually, all decision makers from the Commander in Chief in the White House to the company commander in the field constantly need extensive information concerning the enemy, terrain, and weather. Their desire for information is insatiable. When American soldiers bivouac in a foreign jungle their battalion commanders want to know the strength and location of all enemy forces capable of attacking their men during the night, and rightfully so. Very rapidly the list of their questions fills a book, and since the situation is always changing, the answers to this book of questions must be kept up to date. Old information needs to be corrected as additional information on the questioned period of time becomes known. With modern communications a decision maker in Washington is, in terms of time, just as close to the source of information as is the MACV commander. This poses the danger that decisions will be made on information (unevaluated material) and not on intelligence. Information should be evaluated and analyzed before decisions are made on untimely, inaccurate, or inadequate bases.

Intelligence must be timely. Time is precious. Decisions made on untimely intelligence can result in disaster if the situation has changed. Intelligence should get to the person who can do something about it in time for him to do something. Timely reporting requires extensive, dedicated communications in support of intelligence. Timeliness also is dependent upon effectively written messages. In war, communications are overloaded with questions going back to the originator of information because his initial report was incomplete. Timeliness requires the ability to manipulate data rapidly to assist humans to do the evaluation which only they can do. Computers are a great help, but only that. An automated system of presentation of what a computer "knows" can only reflect a fraction of the data base. The computer data bank must have tremendous storage capacity and programs to permit timely manipulations.

Unless pressure is maintained, promptness will suffer. Each intelligence report should indicate not only distribution made, but when and how each consumer was informed. To insure that highly perishable reports reach commanders promptly, each headquarters should have an individual whose task it is to review the reporting process throughout the intelligence cycle. He must read all reports, not for content but for timeliness. He then must insure that shortcomings are called to the attention of the commanders involved. At J–2, Military Assistance Command, Captain James D. Strachan was responsible for this critical function.

Commanders and staff officers who ask for more information than they need not only delay the receipt of what they need but frequently cannot use what they receive. For example, while I was visiting a division commander he informed me that his division was not receiving requested aerial photography promptly. I immediately looked into his complaint. At that very time, a trailer full of photographs was in his headquarters area. His staff had asked for too much. When it arrived they were too pressed for time to examine the large amount they had requested.

Intelligence must be accurate. Commanders must have confidence in it. Adequate facts must be presented for them to accept the intelligence as valid. Sometimes unverified information leads to wishful thinking. The intelligence officer must be conservative and unshakable in letting the facts speak. Rationalization and crystal ball gazing invite disaster. One either knows the facts or one does not. If one does not, the commander must know that fact.

Intelligence must be adequate. It is not enough to know the location and strength of an enemy. Given only that information a commander might avoid combat because he is outnumbered, even though the enemy is out of ammunition and many of his men are sick.

Intelligence must be usable. First of all, it must be at the lowest classification. It should be unclassified if at all possible so that it can be disseminated easily to all who need it. It should be short. It should be easily understood. It should be limited to essentials. It should be easy to handle and reproduce if required.

It is the job of the intelligence officer at all levels to request or direct the acquisition of information; to collate and evaluate it rapidly; and then to disseminate timely, accurate, adequate, and usable military intelligence to all planners and decision makers. This process may take seconds or days. Such intelligence should permit sound decisions concerning combat operations, war plans, and peace plans. Combat operations should encourage, not negate, negotiations for peace.

Since World War II the U.S. government has put aside its previous naive concept of intelligence and has developed our magnificent intelligence team. This team includes the intelligence organizations of most of the executive departments of the U.S. government. All of these organizations have long ago come of age. They are operated by professionals. I knew that we could depend upon willing support from all members of the team. Many of these agencies were represented on the U.S. team in South Vietnam. Directives existed to ensure proper co-ordination of all functions, and it was my experience over many years that co-operation as well as co-ordination could be expected, but not without strongly held views being expressed by all. Such argument is healthy and necessary for logical co-ordination. However, I was convinced that in time of war the battlefield commander must exercise unity of command in matters of military intelligence. I recommended early that all intelligence within Vietnam be placed under General

Westmoreland, but this recommendation remained in Headquarters, Military Assistance Command.

Our organization had to develop officers who would keep
intelligence "out front," on the initiative. A staff officer who provides intelligence to support operational planning aleardy conceived is actually playing the role of a librarian or a historian. A
staff officer who provides the intelligence that causes orders to be
issued or plans to be made is an intelligence officer. For example,
General Westmoreland had been attending a weekly intelligence
briefing at which a sizable number of his staff was present. The
briefing was primarily an intelligence situation report. Since we
were now at war, such a briefing in my judgment was inadequate.
I changed the scope of the weekly briefing to present an estimate
of enemy capabilities and vulnerabilities, highlighting changes
which had taken place during the week, and at the end of the
briefing made my recommendations as J–2 as to actions the commander should take based upon intelligence. At the end of the
first briefing of this type presented to General Westmoreland early
in August, he asked that the room be cleared of all persons except
a few senior officers. He stated that in the future he wanted the
same type of briefing and he wanted only his component commanders and the chiefs of his staff sections to attend—that this
period would become his strategy session each week.

Another example that took place in August of 1965 was the
result of the J–2 staff's controlling a few resources that were moved
about the country to collect information in support of the commander's strategy and areas of most concern. Through the use of
this resource the location of the 1st Viet Cong Regiment was
learned. As soon as the location was known, a telephone call was
made to headquarters of the U.S. marines. They were given the
information and without delay launched an operation which resulted in the first major encounter between U.S. and Viet Cong
forces in Vietnam, Operation STARLIGHT. Operation CEDAR FALLS
is another example.

People who have not worked in intelligence normally have no
conception of the number of people it takes to perform necessary
activities. Without an extensive data base that can be manipulated
rapidly, it is very difficult to evaluate information and to identify
and ferret out guerrillas and members of the Vietnamese Communist political-military infrastructure. Every scrap of information,
every written report, is to the intelligence officer as nickels and
dimes are to a banker. It takes a lot of them to make the business
profitable. Every piece of information must be accounted for like

money and confirmed or refuted as genuine or counterfeit. When an intelligence analyst receives an unconfirmed report, he cannot let it go. He must confirm or refute it. From numerous reports the order of battle of the enemy is constructed and updated. The enemy order of battle includes his composition, disposition, strength, training status, morale, tactics, logistics, combat effectiveness, and miscellaneous information such as unit histories, personality files, uniforms, and insignias. These factors describing the capabilities and vulnerabilities of an enemy military force can best be learned by gaining access to enemy military personnel who are knowledgeable on the subject or by gaining access to documents they have written.

The most experienced and sophisticated intelligence officers are selected to be estimators. They use order of battle studies, capability studies, and other information to write valid estimates of how the enemy can adversely affect the accomplishment of our mission as well as state enemy vulnerabilities we can exploit. Statements such as "I think," "I believe," or "I feel" must be avoided. The person hearing or reading an estimate should come to the same conclusion as the estimator because of the validity of the intelligence presented and not because of what the estimator thinks.

I had occasion from time to time to tell new estimators of a lesson I learned some years ago on a visit to the advance base of the Summer Institute of Linguistics located deep in the Amazon jungles of Ecuador. A Cofan Indian and his wife were present in the camp. I asked the Indian, through an interpreter, to give me a lesson on how to use his blowgun. He taught me. I asked if he would not prefer to own a rifle. He replied that he used his blowgun to hunt game, especially wild piglets, for his family. He stated that he could blow a poison dart into each of the piglets as they were feeding and after a while pick all of them up, put them in a bag, and take them home, whereas if he used a rifle the noise of the first shot would frighten the pigs away. Furthermore, he would need money to buy the rifle and ammunition, whereas he was able to make his blowgun and darts from the forest. I told this story from time to time to warn my estimators against using an American yardstick to measure other peoples. Even though a guerrilla may not carry a weapon, he certainly knows how to sharpen and replace a pungi stake or to use a hand grenade made from a beer can. A good intelligence officer must avoid preconceived ideas when it comes to estimating the enemy. In Vietnam, it was necessary to discard temporarily many of the conceptions that our military education and experiences had engendered. Our enemy's school was "the bush"—to quote General Giap—and his strategy, tactics, and organization fitted a revised Maoist view of protracted war. For this reason I realized that military intelligence in Vietnam had to adapt if it was to be successful against this enemy.

History records that in time of war the tendency of the U.S. government is to provide the man on the battlefield the resources he needs. The record also reveals repeatedly the sad story of too little too late because we were not prepared. The military also strives to give the commander the resources he needs and furnish him mission-type orders. Because resources seldom are adequate we must retain some under centralized control to be employed in support of the commander's main efforts. We strive for centralized guidance and decentralized operations. History also records that after a war ends resources are greatly reduced, centralized more and more at higher and then higher levels, and given over to civilians to a greater extent. After the Korean War, Army intelligence resources were reduced drastically. In 1965 the resources we needed were not combat ready. Great efforts were made to provide them as quickly as was feasible, but more than two years would be required to receive most of the resources we originally requested. Centralization of scarce resources was continued longer than was desirable.

Even though we were aware that the resources we needed were not readily available, we asked for them. It was up to higher authority to reduce our requests if they had to do so. At this writing I feel only praise for the wholehearted support we received. Time to organize, equip, train, and deploy the units we needed was the bottleneck.

In making our plans I told my staff to think big. I knew that good intelligence requires a sophisticated and large organization. We were at war; this was no time to grow piecemeal. We needed our best effort as soon as possible.

We needed all the help we could get from our Vietnamese allies. They also needed our help. Experience with other allies had taught me that advising them on how to conduct intelligence is not so effective as is working together. Not only does working together develop competence faster, it also engenders mutual respect and confidence. During my initial call on Colonel Ho Van Loi, J–2, Joint General Staff, Republic of Vietnam Armed Forces, and my counterpart and friend for almost two years, I proposed to him that we engage in combined intelligence activities whenever practicable; he agreed.

Evolution of the Military Assistance Command Intelligence Organization

Up to the time the decisions were made to employ U.S. forces and Free World Military Assistance Forces in direct combat operations, the MACV commander's primary means of influencing the conduct and the outcome of the war was through the Military Assistance Program and the advisory effort. Because of limited U.S. participation in combat operations, the scope of Military Assistance Command J–2 activities was also limited. (*Chart 1*) The J–2 mission at that time was to support and improve the Vietnamese military intelligence effort and to keep the Commander, U.S. Military Assistance Command, Vietnam; the Commander in Chief, Pacific; and national intelligence agencies informed on the intelligence situation.

CHART 1—ASSISTANT CHIEF OF STAFF, J–2, STAFF ORGANIZATION, JULY 1965

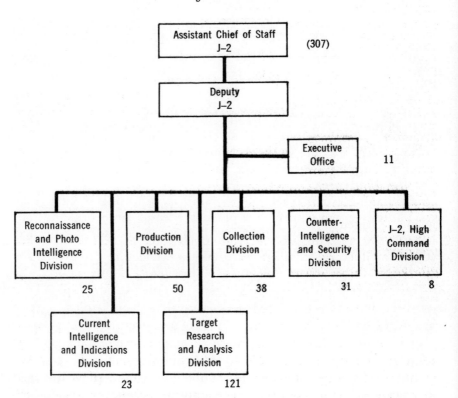

Intelligence reports were received from the advisory system, limited bilateral operations with the Vietnamese clandestine collection organization, the 5th U.S. Special Forces Group, unilateral U.S. military collection resources which included special intelligence activities such as airborne radio direction finding, photo and visual reconnaissance, and infrared and side-looking airborne radar reconnaissance. These resources were provided on a very austere basis.

General Westmoreland now became Commanding General, U.S. Army, Vietnam (USARV), as well as MACV commander. He decided to exercise command from MACV headquarters. It then would be my responsibility to support his strategic planning as well as his tactical operations. I would be not only Military Assistance Command J–2 with the responsibility of exercising general staff supervision over all Army, Navy, Air Force, and Marine Corps intelligence activities, but in addition I would perform those functions of Assistant Chief of Staff for Intelligence, G–2, U.S. Army, Vietnam, required to support tactical operations of the Army. In this role I assumed operational control of Army-level resources as they arrived. Military Assistance Command J–2 continued to be responsible for advising the Republic of Vietnam Armed Forces (RVNAF). The existing organization was not designed to support our new mission and especially this type of war. (*Appendix A*)

According to existing Army doctrine the intelligence force structure is tailored to the organization it supports and, modified by considerations of the enemy, to terrain, weather, mission, and scheme of operations.

The military problem of defeating the North Vietnamese Army and the Viet Cong main force units on the battlefield was complicated by their utilization of a highly centralized political movement. The Viet Cong infrastructure (VCI), composed of men, women, and children, operated as the enemy's supply service, intelligence network, and local guerrilla force as well as a shadow government in each village in Vietnam. If victory on the battlefield was to be translated into a just and lasting peace, the infrastructure had to be neutralized. In order to accomplish this sensitive mission we needed a massive data bank and a staff of sophisticated area specialists. This effort eventually supported the political stabilization of the government of Vietnam and the military activity of Free World Military Assistance Forces. We would need a large countrywide counterintelligence effort involved in countersabotage, countersubversion, and counterespionage activities as well as providing support to all units and installations concerning security of information, personnel, and surreptitious entry. We would need a large, countrywide area intelligence collection effort in order to provide coverage of enemy areas and organizations to collect information as well as to promote defection of enemy personnel.

Our first step was to identify those resources required to support the U.S. Army, Vietnam. Each separate brigade, each division, and each field force (the name given to a corps) would arrive with its normal military intelligence detachment. In addition, one aviation company (aerial surveillance) and a topographic company were requested to support each field force. The aviation companies were equipped with three models of the OV–1 Mohawk aircraft. The number of each model for each company was determined according to the type of terrain and water in the particular field force area of operations.

We provided for U.S. military intelligence detachments to be attached to each South Vietnamese division and corps. We developed the manning requirements for the four original combined centers for intelligence, document exploitation, military interrogation, and materiel exploitation. We increased our requirement for advisers in order to provide specialists down to include all district headquarters. For Military Assistance Command we requested a military intelligence group headquarters (a brigade headquarters did not exist) to command a counterintelligence group, an intelligence group, a military intelligence battalion (air reconnaissance support), and a military intelligence battalion to administer the personnel working in the centers, the advisers, and various support activities. In addition, large numbers of combat troops would be arriving soon, before Military Assistance Command intelligence resources were available. In the interim the war was going on.

The J–2 staff was a large joint one with many qualified people. I decided to reduce the span of control and at the same time increase the number of functions necessary to perform our new mission adequately. An Air Force weather officer was added to the staff. The old Production Division and the Current Intelligence and Indications Division were combined into the Intelligence Division. The Target Research and Analysis Division, as its name implies, was primarily concerned with locating targets for B–52 bombers. I used it as a nucleus to form the Combined Intelligence Center, Vietnam (CICV). (Chart 2) We needed to increase our data base rapidly and our ability to produce capability studies as well as our ability to select targets not only for the B–52's but for

CHART 2—J–2 STAFF ORGANIZATION, OCTOBER 1965

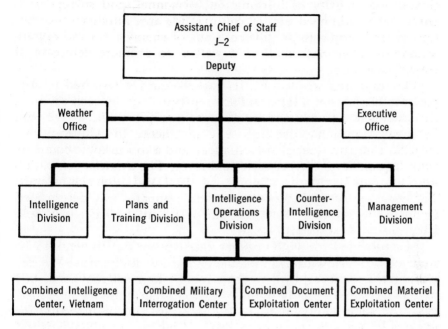

all types of U.S. and Vietnamese Army, Navy, Marine Corps, and Air Force operations. The organizational concept for the Combined Intelligence Center can best be described by using this matrix:

	Area of Intelligence Interest						
Functions	I CTZ Team	II CTZ Team	III CTZ Team	IV CTZ Team	Cambodia Team	Laos Team	North Vietnam Team
Order of Battle							
Imagery Interpretation							
Area Analysis							
Targets							
Technical Intelligence							

Seven teams composed of Vietnamese and Americans were established, one for each of the subareas of intelligence interest. Each team included order of battle, imagery interpretation, area analysis, targets, and technical intelligence specialists or support. The team was our primary data base and production activity. It was placed under the direct supervision of the chief of the Intelligence Division. A plans and training division was created. It was responsible for the preparation of directives and supervision of their execution to ensure proper intelligence training of U.S. and Vietnamese personnel as well as for the preparation of plans involving two or more divisions. The Reconnaissance and Photo Intelligence Division was combined with the Collection Division into the Intelligence Operations Division with many additional combat intelligence functions. The J–2 of the Vietnamese Joint General Staff operated a very small interrogation center in Saigon. I had visited it several times between 1963 and 1965. Colonel Loi and I joined forces and established the Combined Military Interrogation Center (CMIC). The small U.S. effort on documents translation was co-ordinated with the Vietnamese effort to form the Combined Document Exploitation Center (CDEC). When facilities were available these efforts were joined to form the finest documents center I have ever seen. I have always considered the greatest source of information a person who is knowledgeable on the subject and the second greatest source a document containing such information. I took personal interest in all the combined activities, but the Intelligence Center, Interrogation Center, and Document Center received almost daily impetus from me. For this same reorganization I created the Combined Materiel Exploitation Center (CMEC). The Vietnamese placed a few people at this center but operated a facility of their own. Technical intelligence production was done both at the Combined Materiel Exploitation Center and at the Combined Intelligence Center. The Combined Intelligence Center reports were broader in scope. The Military Interrogation, Document Exploitation, and Materiel Exploitation Centers were placed under the direct authority of the chief of the Intelligence Operations Division. The Counterintelligence and Security Division was retained and many additional functions were assigned to it. I created a management division to assist me and my staff in handling the large and sophisticated organization now taking shape. (*Chart 3*)

By May 1967 the authorized strength of my staff had grown from 307 to 467. (*Appendix B*) My request for 166 more people had been forwarded to meet recognized requirements. As my staff

CHART 3—ASSISTANT CHIEF OF STAFF, J-2, STAFF ORGANIZATION, MAY 1967

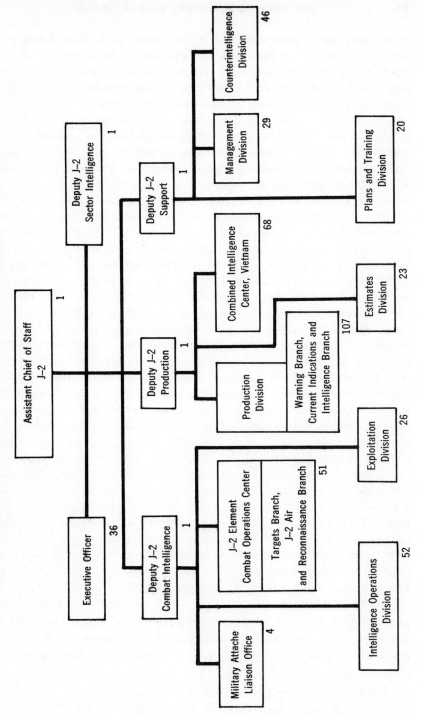

grew in number and functions I kept my span of control small. I insisted that staff memoranda and command directives be written, thoroughly co-ordinated, and published to insure continuity in our activities. I approved all such memoranda and directives. Once they were approved, my chiefs had full authority to implement them.

Since the war in Vietnam was predominantly concerned with combined efforts to defeat the enemy on the ground, the major impact resultant therefrom was upon the U.S. Army military intelligence organization. (*Appendix C*)

The U.S. Army intelligence force available in July 1965 included the 704th Intelligence Corps Detachment, Detachment I of the 500th Intelligence Corps Group, and 218 intelligence advisers who were thinly spread among South Vietnamese corps, divisions, sectors, and special zones. The 704th was a small counterintelligence detachment of forty-six men. It was the counterpart organization to the Republic of Vietnam Military Security Service. It had been under my operational control when I was the U.S. Army, Pacific, G–2. However, I had assigned it to Military Assistance Command, Vietnam. It was also engaged in limited counterespionage, countersabotage, and countersubversion activities. Detachment I of the 500th Intelligence Group had also been under my operational control and was assigned to Military Assistance Command at the same time as the 704th. Detachment I had fifty-six officers and enlisted men. This detachment had a dual role of advising and assisting the South Vietnamese in intelligence collection and engaging in limited collection activities.

Those two detachments were a far cry from what the intelligence force structure should be according to our established doctrine. I knew well such Army doctrine and the capabilities and limitations of all types of U.S. Army intelligence units. As G-2 I had reviewed every U.S. Army, Pacific, contingency plan and had recommended changes in the force structure to support those plans. I had requested a military intelligence battalion to be transferred from the continental United States to Hawaii. This was done. The battalion was reorganized to support the contingency plans better. Part of it was structured to support operations in Vietnam. That detachment was sent in response to my urgent request to assist in establishing the order of battle files for the Combined Intelligence Center. I knew that it would take a year or more for the Department of the Army to activate, train, and deploy to Vietnam new intelligence battalions and groups. However, our organizations were cellular in concept; one could request various functional teams to be attached to existing units. Such individual teams could be created rapidly and their arrival could be programmed over a period of months. I requested such teams. This course of action saved time and spread out the buildup so that no one unit or activity had to turn over all its experienced men at one time.

By June 1967 U.S. Army intelligence units under the operational control of Military Assistance Command J–2 had grown in strength from 102 to 2,466, advisers from 218 to 622. (*Appendix D*) An additional 615 personnel were on request to complete the organization considered essential. Also, the completed staff action of a new table of organization and equipment for a U.S. Army intelligence brigade to be commanded by a brigadier general had been submitted.

The 525th Military Intelligence Group was under the command of the Commanding General, U.S. Army, Vietnam (General Westmoreland), and under my operational control. The commanding officer of the 525th Military Intelligence Group exercised command over a signal company, an aviation detachment, and the 135th Military Intelligence Group (Counterintelligence), which absorbed the mission and assets of its predecessor, the 704th Intelligence Corps Detachment. (*Chart 4*) The 135th was organized into six regions, was dispersed throughout South Vietnam, and was located in most places along with the Vietnamese Military Security Service. The 149th Military Intelligence Group (Collection) absorbed the mission and assets of its predecessor, Detachment I of the 500th Intelligence Group; the 1st Military Intelligence Battalion (Air Reconnaissance Support), which had the mission of interpreting, reproducing, and delivering Air Force imagery flown in support of ground tactical commanders; and the 519th Military Intelligence Battalion, which provided the personnel and support for the combined centers.

In 1965 U.S. intelligence advisory sections with South Vietnamese corps and divisions were inadequately manned and unable to process the increased flow of intelligence information into U.S. channels; they also had difficulty providing requisite support to Vietnamese corps and division G–2's. To alleviate this problem the U.S. advisory sections with Vietnamese corps and divisions were reorganized as military intelligence detachments with greatly increased manning. In addition, manning levels of special zone and sector advisory teams were increased. The current adviser element reflects an authorized manning level of 621 as compared with the previous level of 218.

CHART 4—525TH MILITARY INTELLIGENCE GROUP

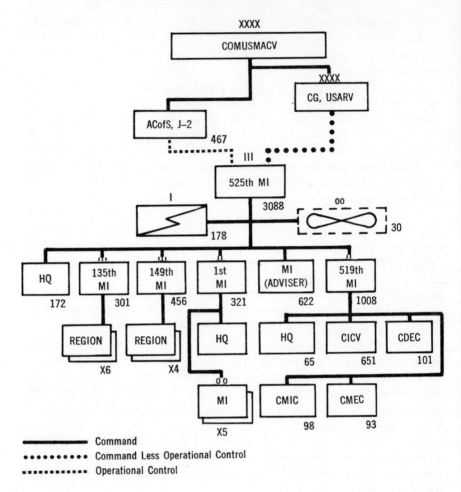

We have only taken a glance at the over-all MACV intelligence organization. In order to keep this monograph unclassified I have omitted much. Such information is available in other records for those who are authorized to have it. But I would be remiss if I did not at least mention that special intelligence played a major role. As Military Assistance Command J–2 I exercised operational control over much of the effort of special intelligence personnel even though they were shown as being in direct support of the MACV commander. This was done with the full approval of the authorities in Washington.

CHAPTER II

Combined Intelligence

The Combined Intelligence Concept

Americans and South Vietnamese were fighting together on the same battlefield against a common enemy. Both of us needed the same intelligence on the enemy, the terrain, and the weather. Each of us had capabilities and limitations affecting our ability to collect and produce the needed intelligence. We Americans would add trained and experienced men, sophisticated equipment, money, professionalism, management techniques, rapid communications, a sense of urgency, and the support of our intelligence team. On the other hand, we had very few linguists who could speak Vietnamese. We were invited to assist the Vietnamese and, as guests of their country, were subject to their sovereignty.

The South Vietnamese were sovereign. They controlled sources of information, real estate, and archives. They had many years of experience in fighting this type of war. They had an insight into the thinking of enemy leaders, they had an understanding and appreciation of enemy tactics and modus operandi, and they knew what information was available in their files and archives and could make it available. They would add continuity to our common activities because they remained when we Americans went home after serving our tours of duty. They spoke the same language as the enemy.

They also had some limitations. They did not have enough trained intelligence officers and specialists. They lacked necessary equipment and money. Together we could be a strong team.

Combined intelligence was not a new concept with me. I had practiced it on much smaller scales before. I had experienced first-hand the value of international co-operation in intelligence operations as General George S. Patton's chief of intelligence in Germany after World War II when thousands of refugees had to be screened, in Greece in 1949–1950 during the successful counterinsurgency there, and in various other countries where U.S. intelligence worked in concert with local intelligence agencies.

During my initial call on Colonel Loi, I discussed our capabilities and limitation and proposed that we create a combined intelligence system with activities at all levels of command. He enthusiastically agreed. The concept envisioned the United States forces working not merely in an advisory role, but side by side with the Republic of Vietnam Armed Forces as equals in a partnership. In the system we would establish centers throughout the country for interrogation of prisoners and *Hoi Chanhs* and for exploitation of captured documents and materiel as well as a center where all information would be sent for collation, analysis, evaluation, and processing into intelligence in support of U.S. and South Vietnam forces. Combined training would be conducted to familiarize U.S. and South Vietnamese personnel with each other's intelligence procedures and techniques; there would be an exchange of Army of the Republic of Vietnam (ARVN) and U.S. military intelligence detachments at all levels down to separate brigade.

The combined concept was founded in mutual need, trust, and understanding. The Vietnamese had to know that the United States was working openly with them. In turn, I had to dispel the criticism some Americans voiced implying apathy on the part of our counterparts. Unlike the U.S. advisers who would be in the country only one year, the Vietnamese were permanently committed in their homeland. We were obligated to work a seven-day week; we had, essentially, nothing else to do. The Vietnamese had been under the pressure of fighting a war for years. They had families to rear and care for. They could not match our schedules or initial energy year after year under pressure, but they were on the job around the clock if needed.

Attention to detail in every regard was necessary for success of the combined concept. The combined centers were to have codirectors (U.S. and Vietnamese) occupying adjoining offices. Daily visits and command supervision at all levels were in order. A positive approach was taken by all concerned. Before U.S. personnel were assigned to any of the combined centers, an orientation program was mandatory and we stressed continual reeducation. Daily fifteen-minute language classes, conducted for Americans with the objective of improving our capability, served as evidence of our sincerity to assist the Republic of Vietnam. In addition, all briefings and charts were bilingual. As sophisticated equipment arrived, the Vietnamese were taught to operate and maintain it, and eventually the computers were programmed bilingually to include diacritical marks. Vietnamese and Americans performed the same tasks together, be it reviewing an agent report or a computer printout or answering a request from a combat unit. The combined approach offered a continuity of effort and direction as well as an opportunity to learn from the Vietnamese while they learned from us.

As the U.S. role increased, as our intelligence requirements grew in complexity, the need for definitive political and diplomatic agreements began to surface. The sovereignty of the government of Vietnam had to be protected by the military intelligence community. We found that technically we lacked the authority to accomplish many of our intelligence functions. How were we to handle prisoners? What disposition was to be made of captured documents and materiel? This was not a declared war. We were there not as a conquering army or liberation force; we were in South Vietnam to help the people win a war and build a nation. Their sovereignty was inviolate.

Consequently, much work had to be done to prepare necessary agreements, not only between Military Assistance Command and the government of Vietnam but including all the Free World forces. An important lesson to be learned from our experiences in Vietnam is that we should have within the intelligence community samples of agreements that might be necessary on such activities as the handling of prisoners of war, the release of classified information, and combined intelligence activities. The formal agreements were made not solely to assign specific responsibilities; they were a means of providing continuity and increasing efficiency. They also contained manning and staffing requirements and explained command and control channels. A separate agreement was negotiated for each of the combined activities. While all were similar as to administrative procedures, each had distinct aspects:

In addition to complying with the Geneva Convention, each signatory of the agreement establishing the Combined Military Interrogation Center agreed to turn over to the center as soon as possible any significant or important prisoner. As for the Combined Materiel Exploitation Center, priority on captured materiel was assigned to the Republic of Vietnam Armed Forces. Any time a new piece of enemy materiel was captured, the first model was released to the South Vietnamese after exploitation for display in their museum. The second model went to the United States for further tests and evaluation. Subsequent pieces were returned to the capturing unit, or if they were of a type used by our allies they could be returned to supply channels. The agreement for the Combined Document Exploitation Center stipulated that the government of Vietnam retain ownership of all captured documents, currency, and publications of all types.

Since the United States provided a large portion of the financial support of all the Free World forces, it was only to be expected that some formal arrangements for accountability of funds be established. In the intelligence field, the MACV J–2 agreed to provide contingency funds but retained authority to approve all projects for which funds were requested and to monitor such projects and receive reports that resulted from them. Recipients would be required to maintain detailed fiscal records and submit them for audit by a J–2 representative.

Another important agreement concerned the employment of South Vietnamese Army intelligence detachments with U.S. units. The significant aspects were the organization of the detachments, command relationships, logistical support, and administration.

The Military Intelligence Detachment Exchange Program

The Military Intelligence Detachment Exchange Program was implemented to improve combat intelligence in U.S., South Vietnamese, and Free World Military Assistance Forces tactical units. Regardless of the language barrier, the attachment of U.S. detachments to South Vietnamese divisions provided the Vietnamese commanders with special skills and technical expertise not normally available and, as a bonus, afforded an excellent channel through which pertinent information could be forwarded to the J–2, Military Assistance Command. Of particular interest to this report, however, are the benefits derived from the attachment of South Vietnamese detachments to U.S. corps-level headquarters, divisions, and separate brigades.

The program began officially in January 1966 with the signing of an agreement by the United States and Republic of Vietnam Armed Forces. (Later both the Korean and Australian forces negotiated similar agreements.) To facilitate implementation and promote compatibility, the South Vietnamese military intelligence detachments were to be organized in accordance with the table of organization and equipment of a U.S. military intelligence detachment organic to airborne and Marine brigades. (*Appendix E*). At full strength such a detachment consists of eight officers, eighteen noncommissioned officers, and four enlisted men comprising a headquarters, prisoner of war interrogation (IPW) section, order of battle (OB) section, imagery interpretation (II) section, and document analysis section. Even though the Vietnamese intelligence school in Cho Lon was operating at full capacity in order to provide intelligence specialists, the Republic of Vietnam Armed Forces was short of trained intelligence personnel, and reduced-strength detachments had to be formed and deployed to avoid excessive delays in initiating the program. Particular emphasis was placed on obtaining additional interrogators and documents analysts. As detachments became operational, assignments were made in accordance with J–2 priorities.

Upon joining a U.S. unit, the South Vietnamese detachment normally was integrated with the organic intelligence detachment, complementing it with skilled intelligence specialists who were proficient linguists knowledgeable in local dialects, customs, and habits. Their ability to analyze captured documents or interrogate prisoners on the spot enabled commanders immediately to exploit information of tactical significance. As the Vietnamese became more proficient, they enhanced the timeliness of local intelligence by rapidly culling the unimportant and identifying those that merited further processing. Indeed, units without Vietnamese support often contributed to the overload of the exploitation system by forwarding volumes of meaningless documents.

Continuity proved to be an enduring benefit made possible by having Vietnamese elements with the U.S. units. The rapid turnover of U.S. soldiers hindered the development and main-tenance of intimate familiarity with the enemy and the local area. The permanence of the Vietnamese detachment greatly alleviated the problem. This benefit carried over into civil affairs and relations with local agencies where in several instances the Vietnamese personnel played a leading role in establishing rapport with the Regional Forces and Popular Forces, National Police, sector officials, and other government authorities.

The exchange program was the subject of some controversy, and not all our intelligence officers considered it either worthwhile or desirable. Difficulties arose because of language barriers, the difference in customs and habits, and the relatively short tenure of U.S. intelligence personnel. Over-all, the program justified its existence, though it would be inaccurate to say that every G–2 was satisfied with his Vietnamese detachment. Most G–2's who conscientiously integrated the Vietnamese unit into their intelli-gence apparatus enjoyed outstanding success in accomplishing missions and satisfying requirements levied by their commanders.

By May 1967, and with the exception of the 11th Armored Cavalry Regiment, 196th and 199th Light Infantry Brigades, and the Republic of Korea Marine Brigade, all U.S. and Free World forces had Vietnamese military intelligence units assigned.

Vietnamese units were being trained for the other organizations and were assigned later in the year.

The Combined Interrogation System

Establishment of an effective program for the interrogation of enemy prisoners and *Hoi Chanhs* was a high priority objective. At a briefing for Secretary McNamara in July of 1965, I presented my plan calling for the construction of military interrogation centers at each division, sector, and corps, along with a national center at Saigon. This plan was co-ordinated with embassy representatives, who agreed, with the exception of interrogation centers at sector level. They considered these centers more closely related to the police effort than to the military and consequently thought they should be constructed by civil authority. I accepted this proposal with the understanding that facilities within the sector centers would be available for use by military interrogators. An embassy representative accompanied me to Secretary McNamara's briefing and acknowledged this commitment. The secretary approved the plan and directed that it be implemented.

The agreement for a combined intelligence exploitation system provided for interrogation of captives and returnees. In consonance with its terms, the Combined Military Interrogation Center (CMIC) was established in Saigon and became the focal point of tactical and strategic exploitation of selected human sources. (*Chart 5*) As with the other exploitation programs, Americans and Vietnamese working together in a spirit of co-operation and mutual support carried out the combined interrogation activities. The success we achieved with this program is a tribute to the outstanding performance of duty of Major Lawrence Sutton, Lieutenant Colonel Frederick A. Pieper, and Captain Lam Van Nghia, who were instrumental in making the center operational. The system promoted maximum utilization of available resources and facilitated the exchange of sources and interrogation reports, allowing cross-servicing of requirements. Perhaps the greatest benefits accrued to the United States since a persistent shortage of trained, Vietnamese-speaking interrogators had seriously curtailed American efforts to exploit human sources. As a result of the combined concept, the over-all interrogation effort profited as the native fluence of the South Vietnamese was complemented by U.S. technical expertise. Many of our highly qualified interrogators learned Vietnamese at the language school in Monterey. Sergeant Sedgewick Tourison deserves special mention. His professionalism and dedication to duty were consistently outstanding. He proved to

CHART 5—ORGANIZATION, COMBINED MILITARY INTERROGATION CENTER, MAY 1967

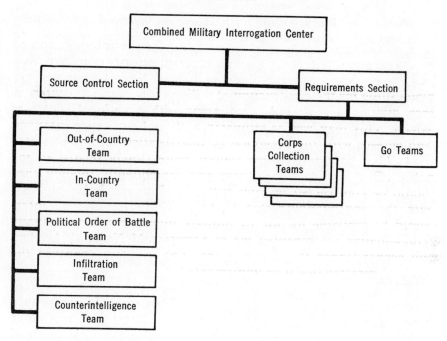

be invaluable in key interrogations on numerous occasions, an important example of which was his detailed interrogation of nineteen Vietnamese naval personnel picked up in the Gulf of Tonkin after their patrol craft was sunk. As of 15 May 1966, the Combined Military Interrogation Center had a total of ten U.S. language-qualified interrogators. I was also fortunate to have an excellent linguist in my special assistant, Captain James D. Strachan, who was the honor graduate of the 1964 Vietnamese language course at the Defense Language Institute, West Coast Branch.

The Combined Military Interrogation Center personnel complement consisted of an Army of the Republic of Vietnam and a U.S. element, both headed by directors with equal authority in the operation of the center. Operational control of the center emanated from both J–2, Military Assistance Command, and J–2, Republic of Vietnam Armed Forces Joint General Staff. (*Appendix F*) We organized the center along functional lines, simplifying the definition of responsibilities and expediting processing of captives and detainees.

A source control section was created to facilitate selection of sources to be brought to Saigon. It reviewed preliminary interrogation reports submitted by lower echelons in order to identify knowledgeable sources. This evaluation went to the Requirements Branch which selected the interrogatees to be evacuated to the Combined Military Interrogation Center. During the first four months of 1967 the center distributed 675 interrogation reports and 1,068 intelligence information reports. Each interrogation report was reproduced in 350 copies and sent to 92 different addresses worldwide.

The Requirements Branch was the nerve center of combined interrogation. Based on specific intelligence collection requirements generated by units throughout the country and validated by J–2, Military Assistance Command, the branch matched these requirements to knowledgeable sources. They briefed the appropriate requirements team on what they knew concerning the source, and finally they insured that all requirements had been satisfied before authorizing termination of an interrogation. The Requirements Branch supervised five requirements teams, each specializing in particular intelligence requirements. They knew what we knew and they knew what we needed to know. One team sought information about the enemy order of battle outside Vietnam. Another was concerned with order of battle within the country. Enemy tactics, weapons, equipment, psychological operations, and political order of battle (the enemy infrastructure) fell within the purview of a third team. A fourth team focused on counterintelligence: sabotage, espionage, and subversion directed against allied facilities or men. The fifth team concentrated on enemy infiltration. The members of the requirements teams briefed the interrogators and furnished the questions to be asked.

Interrogation reports published by the Combined Military Interrogation Center received wide distribution. Since sources interrogated in Saigon normally already had been exploited for any "hot" information before reaching the center, these reports seldom contained perishable intelligence. If the need arose, however, spot reports of immediate interest were transmitted electrically. A daily summary advised the intelligence community (including Washington) of the type of information obtained from the sources on hand. Knowledgeability briefs, too, were dispatched to interested parties announcing the availability of each source and his area of expertise.

The Combined Military Interrogation Center stationed collection teams with each corps and throughout South Vietnam. "Go" teams composed of U.S. and South Vietnamese interrogators were always ready to be dispatched from Saigon to support combat units when interrogation requirements exceeded local capabilities. These teams were especially valuable during sweep operations that resulted in multitudes of detainees who had to be given at least a cursory check in order to detect exploitable sources.

Evacuation of prisoners flowed normally from the capturing unit to the brigade or division detention area where tactical interrogation could be accomplished. Subsequent transferrals to the local Vietnamese interrogation facility or evacuations to the U.S. corps combined center depended on the captive's knowledge. This factor also influenced further channeling to the Combined Military Interrogation Center or the government's national interrogation center (if he had nonmilitary information) for thorough interrogation. After completing the interrogation process, the captive was placed in a detention center. Expeditious processing was stressed at all levels of command, and each echelon was encouraged to limit interrogations to information in satisfaction of local requirements. Seven days was the maximum time any element below the Combined Military Interrogation Center was authorized to detain a captive.

A preliminary interrogation report reflecting highlights of the field interrogation was submitted through channels to the combined center via J–2, Military Assistance Command. Reports of any subsequent interrogations also were distributed to higher and adjacent commands. They included pertinent biographic data, the circumstances of capture, areas of special knowledge, and an assessment by the interrogation team of the source's physical condition, intelligence, and co-operativeness.

Returnees (ralliers or *Hoi Chanhs*) usually were transferred by the acquiring unit to the nearest *Chieu Hoi* center or government agency. If the returnee had information of intelligence value, he might be evacuated for interrogation through the same channels as captives but was afforded special treatment to demonstrate the benevolence of the United States and the government of Vietnam and to elicit his co-operation. Within the combined centers, ralliers had separate dormitories and mess halls and were placed under very few restrictions. As soon as his interrogation was completed, the returnee was housed in the *Chieu Hoi* center of his choice. If a returnee was questioned within a *Chieu Hoi* center, we ordinarily worked openly in a lounge or mess hall and we emphasized winning

RETURNEES WERE SEPARATED FROM PRISONERS *and given greater freedom while being interrogated.*

his co-operation. In the case of very important captives or returnees, the system was flexible enough to permit expeditious processing, enabling the source to reach an appropriate level, usually the combined center, for timely interrogation.

One such source, Le Xuan Chuyen, chief of operations of the Viet Cong 5th Division, defected as a result of one of our counterintelligence operations and was given a private office at the Combined Military Interrogation Center. Chuyen came under government control in Binh Thuan Province, and in order to get him to Saigon as soon as possible, Captain Strachan co-ordinated a U–21 aircraft en route with an empty seat. The "red carpet" treatment was given to Chuyen, whose seat on the plane was opposite that of Lieutenant General John A. Heintges, Deputy Commander, U.S. Military Assistance Command, Vietnam.

During my tour as J–2, Military Assistance Command, I insisted that the interrogation program comply rigidly with the provisions of the Geneva Convention. Abuse by individual Vietnamese, however, did occur. The French and mandarin heritage of brutality died hard, especially in the field, despite the efforts of more enlightened American and Vietnamese officers. Further, many

RETURNEES WERE NORMALLY INTERROGATED IN AN INFORMAL SETTING, *in this case a mess tent.*

members of the Viet Cong infrastructure were not classified as prisoners of war and were interrogated by the National Police, a civil organization which was tasked with the neutralization of antigovernment sentiment. At the Combined Military Interrogation Center, the requirements of the Geneva Convention were observed and prisoners were treated humanely. Vietnamese interrogators exhibited commendable finesse in questioning prisoners. By virtue of their common language and national heritage, they were successful in establishing rapport with prisoners who only hours before may have been enemy soldiers.

I designed the Combined Military Interrogation Center building to include a combined classroom facility. Vietnamese and U.S. soldiers from all over Vietnam here received interrogation training which included the provisions of the Geneva Convention. Any form of maltreatment of sources was strictly taboo.

The Interrogation Center maintained close liaison with the other combined centers. The analyst in the Combined Intelligence Center needed to keep the appropriate requirements teams at the Interrogation Center informed on his intelligence needs. He, in turn, needed to be kept informed on the potential of available

A QUALIFIED U.S. INTERROGATOR WHO CANNOT SPEAK VIETNAMESE *questions a source with the help of a Vietnamese WAC interpreter.*

sources. Each member of the combined intelligence system needed to know how he could help other centers and how they could help him.

Combined Document Exploitation

Before 1 October 1965, document exploitation was primarily a function of the Republic of Vietnam Armed Forces. Our participation was limited to an advisory role since we had only a small translation pool of approximately eight U.S. military personnel and thirty Vietnamese civilians. The main weakness in the effort was the absence of documents to be translated. Vietnamese soldiers had not been imbued with the need to locate and evacuate enemy documents. When they did send some to their headquarters, the documents were kept and not forwarded. Documents are an excellent source of intelligence, second only to a knowledgeable person. I had had much experience in World War II, and later, concerning acquisition and exploitation of documents. I had visited these activities throughout South Vietnam over two years and knew the potential. I had recommended to my predecessors the enlargement of this important source of information. Now we had to have it.

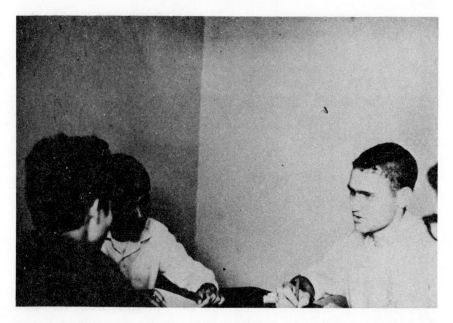

INTERROGATORS RECEIVED TRAINING *by sitting in on interrogations and by conducting interrogations under the tutelage of qualified personnel.*

I sent for Lieutenant Colonel Henry Ajima. He and I had worked together, and I considered him the most competent officer in the Army on the subject. During a period of temporary duty with me in Saigon we made detailed plans, including the written job description for every civilian employee who was to be hired. Colonel Ajima left with the understanding that as soon as the facility which he and I designed was ready he would join my staff to be a codirector of the new Combined Document Exploitation Center.

In the meantime we started hiring people. We wrote the necessary directives. We stimulated the flow of documents. And I requested the Defense Intelligence Agency to train a team of specialists on the intelligence subject code and assign them to me. This was done.

I also requested that an FMA document storage and retrieval package along with a civilian technician and a civilian maintenance man be delivered as soon as possible. They arrived in a short time and set up trial operations in one of my offices. When the building was ready Colonel Ajima arrived and we moved in. We were in business. This center turned out to be of unsurpassed value.

The Combined Document Exploitation Center opened at

its location near the Tan Son Nhut air base on 24 October 1966, implementing the agreement between the Commander, U.S. Military Assistance Command, Vietnam, and the chief of the Joint General Staff for the conduct of combined intelligence activities. (*Chart 6*) The center was assigned the mission of supporting allied military operations by receiving and exploiting captured enemy documents, co-ordinating the over-all joint document exploitation effort, and providing field support teams, translation, and document storage and retrieval services. The center had five major functional elements with an authorized strength of over three hundred U.S. and South Vietnamese military personnel as well as Vietnamese civilians.

From July 1966 to May 1967 the center received well in excess of three million pages of enemy documents. Approximately one-third of this input was the result of Operation CEDAR FALLS in January 1967, followed by Operation JUNCTION CITY in February. These two operations accounted for nearly one million pages of enemy documents processed by the center. Of this total input, approximately 10 percent was summarized or fully translated into English for distribution to interested agencies. Experience proves that of any batch of documents acquired on the battlefield, at least 10 percent contain information of definite intelligence value.

CHART 6—ORGANIZATION, COMBINED DOCUMENT EXPLOITATION CENTER, MAY 1967

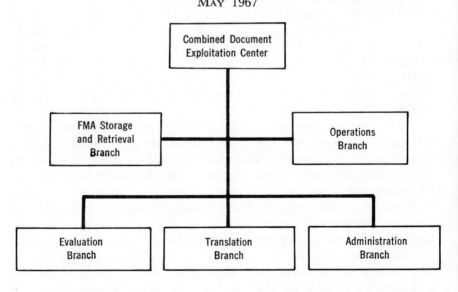

INNER COMPOUND AT CMIC, *where prisoners were detained and interrogated. Each room had a dutch door which was left open during interrogations to discourage mistreatment of prisoners.*

The document exploitation process began at the center immediately upon receipt of documents from capturing units. Generally, documents arrived at the center neatly packaged and tagged with details of the capture including date, place, circumstances, and identity of the capturing unit. During major military operations, however, documents were delivered to the center in every conceivable type of container—bags, boxes, cans, quarter-ton trailers and trucks. Many tactical units delivered documents within hours after capture. During Operations CEDAR FALLS and JUNCTION CITY, documents were received from tactical units as quickly as eight to ten hours after capture, with exploitation being completed within twenty-four hours after capture. If tactical units were unable to deliver documents to the center, then fully equipped combined field teams from the center joined the units to help exploit the documents on the spot.

Initially, documents were carefully screened by highly qualified Vietnamese civilians assigned to the Evaluation Branch. Many of these examiners were retired or demobilized military personnel, such as Captain Sang, who served as the deputy director of the Vietnamese element of the center until his demobilization in April 1967, or Captain Loi, a former member of the G–2 Section, Vietnamese IV Corps. During the screening, in which the Vietnamese element also participated, the documents were divided into five distinct categories to establish priorities for exploitation as well as disposition:

Category Alpha, or Type A, documents required immediate processing, with results being returned to tactical units without delay in the form of a spot report. An example would be an enemy operation plan for an ambush of a friendly element. In these instances the urgency of the information dictated the use of the "hot line" telephone system available to the center for notification to the unit concerned.

The Type Bravo documents contained information of strategic intelligence value such as Viet Cong certificates of commendation, which contained names of Viet Cong as well as unit identification, or a notebook containing information as to the composition, strength, or disposition of an enemy unit. Most of the documents processed through the center were of the B category. All such documents were quickly summarized into English and clearly identified with a permanent document log number.

The Type Charlie documents were those considered to be of marginal intelligence value, such as an enemy-produced sketch map of Africa. These documents were passed to the South Vietnamese element of the center without further processing.

The Type Delta documents were generally propaganda materials such as an English-language document encouraging U.S. troops to write to such organizations as the Students for a Democratic Society (SDS). This category of documents also included currencies of all types, such as North Vietnamese currency. The propaganda materials were forwarded to the appropriate psychological warfare agencies, while the currency was forwarded to the appropriate custodian.

The Type Echo documents contained cryptographic or other information on the enemy communications system, such as the training manual on wire communications. These were passed to the appropriate signal intelligence agency without further processing at the center.

The Alpha and Bravo documents were then routed to another group of highly qualified document specialists who prepared the actual summaries of each document. Those documents which contained detailed information beyond the scope of a summary or

CDEC TRANSLATORS

gist translation were so identified and routed to the Translation Branch for full translation. All such documents had already been summarized, so the time element for full translation was not always a critical factor.

The translators represented the largest single group of highly trained language specialists in Vietnam. Most of them, having acquired a basic knowledge of English in their normal academic training, underwent specialized translator training with the civilian personnel office. Upon employment at the Combined Document Exploitation Center, these translators were placed on a six-month on-the-job training cycle. Such training was emphasized because the Viet Cong, with their propensity for cover names, codes, and jargon, had developed a separate language, unintelligible to the average Vietnamese. From necessity we developed refernce books such as the Dictionary of Viet Cong Terminology required by our translators. Upon completion of the summary or full translation process, documents were immediately forwarded to the Typing Section of the Administrative Branch. Because our typists did not speak, read, or write English, their work had to be closely checked by a group of U.S. military personnel. Then, all documents were routed into the Reproduction Section. During 1966 it was a big day when 100 pounds of reports were printed. By early 1967 the daily volume averaged 1,400 pounds of reports, with every indication of greater volume in the future.

To permit faster response to intelligence requirements the center had the most up-to-date equipment, such as the multilith platemaster, which photographs and develops masters to be used on the multilith press, which prints at the rate of 6,000 pages per hour; and the collator-stitcher, which automatically assemblies and staples each report. Reports then went into the distribution point for Army Post Office or courier delivery to interested agencies. Average time for each report from beginning to end was roughly six hours.

As soon as the master copy of a document summary or full translation entered the Reproduction Section, the original Viet Cong documents and the English translation were diverted to the FMA Document Storage and Retrieval Branch. The first step was the detailed indexing of each report by the team of highly trained U.S. intelligence analysts. The indexing system used was the intelligence subject code. Here, every name, unit identification, place name, and document or report number that appeared in the report was recorded for retrieval purposes. The next step was keypunching the index data on the flexowriters. This equipment produced an index card associated with the FMA system as well as an index tape. Then the index card, the English translation, and the original document were recorded on 35-mm. microfilm. For retrieval, the highly sensitive but dependable FMA equipment was used: A question is entered into the machine by use of a request card; the card is inserted into the retrieval unit and when the search button is pressed, the machine begins an electronic search at the rate of 6,400 pages per minute; each time a frame appears that answers the question, the machine projects an 8x10-inch image of that report on a screen. The machine can make hard copies in five seconds. Document reports, interrogation reports, agent reports, and Military Assistance Command intelligence summaries were indexed and entered into the system. To permit greater access to this data base, the system also provided answers to queries in the form of microfilm strips and 16-mm. film which could be used by the requester on film reader printers which were made available to all headquarters.

To provide efficient use of the data base, this system was interfaced with the IBM 1401 computer located at the Combined Intelligence Center. The link was provided by the IBM 047 converter which converted the document indexing data from the index tape into IBM card format. These IBM cards, which contained all indexing data, were then programmed into the 1401 computer. This provided the intelligence producers with complete data regarding the availability of information on a specific unit or subject.

At this point the original documents, which were the legal property of the Republic of Vietnam, were passed to the Vietnamese document archives which was also located in the combined facility. Here, files of selected Viet Cong documents dating back to January 1962 were available for perusal by the intelligence community.

To assist national intelligence agencies and staff sections, the center's complete 35-mm. microfilm data base was furnished Pacific Command and the Defense Intelligence Agency and was updated continually. Personnel of the center periodically visited major headquarters in Vietnam to photograph their intelligence files and reduce them to 16-mm. microfilm cartridge format for permanent retention. Since captured enemy documents legally remained Vietnamese property, the Vietnamese complement at the Combined Document Exploitation Center comprised the national archives for such material.

"Go" teams from the center were available to aid in screening large amounts of documents captured or uncovered during combat operations, but often there was just too much material for the teams to translate. Before teams were dispatched we encouraged sending such materials by special courier to the center, where document exploitation was much more efficient. Most commands followed this procedure.

In the tactical units, personnel in the interrogation sections processed captured documents in addition to conducting prisoner interrogations and administrative functions. Documents obtained during combat operations usually were forwarded directly to brigade where a small U.S. and Vietnamese team screened them for information of immediate tactical value and issued spot reports on critical or perishable items. On some operations an interrogation team accompanied battalion-size units, and the initial screening and readouts were done at that level. The documents then were passed to the division or separate brigade authorities for more detailed processing. At division level, document processing was more thorough; however, emphasis was placed on getting the documents back to the combined center as quickly as possible.

Document evacuation policies were not uniform; human factors combined with physical elements resulted in procedural variances.

Some units, such as the 25th Infantry Division in Cu Chi, were close enough to Saigon to send daily couriers to the center. The 1st Air Cavalry Division and the 11th Armored Cavalry Regiment often used helicopters for quick transfer from the capturing unit to higher headquarters. It was preferred that the tactical units send documents to the center for full translation rather than tie up their organic interpreters and translators. Experience showed that the Combined Document Exploitation Center could, by far, provide the most rapid readouts, summaries, and full or extract translations of significant documents. When we discovered that some units were delaying transfer of certain documents until they could complete local exploitation, we procured duplicating machines so that units could copy documents they wished to retain and send the originals back to the center. This simple measure permitted significant improvements in our document exploitation system.

The objective of the Combined Document Exploitation Center, as well as the Combined Military Interrogation Center and the Combined Materiel Exploitation Center, was to provide the data base essential to intelligence production organizations such as the Combined Intelligence Center.

Combined Materiel Exploitation

In August 1965, the Military Assistance Command technical intelligence capability was limited. The collection and examination of captured materiel was done as little more than additional duty as time and work load permitted. From this austere beginning a sophisticated, efficient materiel exploitation program evolved. We designed a suitable organization, requisitioned the necessary specialists, and prepared the requisite MACV directives to establish the materiel exploitation system based upon a formal agreement between Military Assistance Command and Republic of Vietnam Armed Forces. Qualified technical intelligence personnel were few. Again we taught special classes and conducted on-the-job training for fillers while the few experienced, qualified specialists who had been developed in the country sought to get on with the war. Majors Donald D. Rhode and John C. Baker and Vietnamese Army Major Van Lam played key roles in the development of the Combined Materiel Exploitation Center, and through their efforts command technical intelligence grew rapidly and efficiently.

The Combined Materiel Exploitation Center was charged with collecting and exploiting captured materiel of all types, and this entailed examination, identification, analysis, evaluation of the items, and dissemination of the intelligence obtained. We needed to determine the characteristics, capabilities, and limitations of enemy materiel and equipment so that adequate countermeasures could be devised. The center tailored its organization for the Vietnam environment in an effort to realize maximum exploitation. (*Chart 7*) The Graphics Section provided illustrator and photographic support; the Laboratory performed chemical analysis to determine the composition of unidentified substances; Receiving and Shipping received materiel from capturing units and prepared selected items for shipment to the United States; the Communications-Electronics Section exploited all signal equipment, including electronic and photography items; the Mobility Section evaluated and analyzed enemy mines, booby traps, engineer items, transportation equipment, construction, and barrier materials; the Weapons and Munitions Section analyzed fragments to determine the type of ammunition employed; the Medical Section evaluated enemy medical supplies, equipment, medical capabilities, and noneffective rates due to medical causes among enemy units; and the General

CHART 7—ORGANIZATION, COMBINED MATERIEL EXPLOITATION CENTER

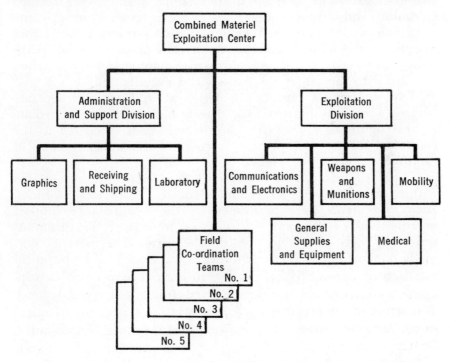

Supply and Equipment Section evaluated and analyzed enemy clothing, individual equipment, rations, petroleum products, and chemical, bacteriological, and radiological equipment.

Specific intelligence collection requirements listing items of enemy materiel for which the intelligence community had a need were prepared by the Combined Materiel Exploitation Center and published by J–2, Military Assistance Command, to provide collection guidance to field commanders. When captured or otherwise obtained, items of command interest were reported expeditiously through intelligence channels to J–2, Military Assistance Command, while the materiel itself was tagged by the capturing unit and evacuated to the center for full-scale exploitation. Items of captured materiel determined to be of immediate tactical importance were spot reported through channels and the center dispatched a "go" team to effect immediate exploitation. The lack of experienced technical intelligence personnel hindered exploitation by U.S. units below division and separate brigade. The unit's primary responsibility concerned the recovery and evacuation of materiel from the capture site to the nearest maintenance collecting point, except for food and medical supplies which were handled separately and explosive items that were evacuated through ammunition supply channels. When evacuation was impossible, either because of the tactical situation or the size of the item, all pertinent data were recorded and, along with photographs or sketches, forwarded to the center for analysis and examination.

Exploitation of captured materiel at division and separate brigade level was limited to a determination of the immediate tactical significance, and the materiel was then evacuated to the combined center. The prompt evacuation of significant items of captured materiel was stressed.

Captured materiel was channeled to collecting points located within each area support command of the corps tactical zones. Such movements were performed by the maintenance support organizations of the capturing unit or by support organizations providing logistical services within the corps. The materiel normally remained at each echelon until it was examined by technical intelligence personnel. Except for authorized war trophies, captured materiel could not be removed from Military Assistance Command or otherwise disposed of until released by technical intelligence personnel of the Combined Materiel Exploitation Center.

Screening and preliminary field exploitation of captured materiel was done by field co-ordination teams that normally operated

MATERIEL OF INTEREST TO THE GENERAL SUPPLY AND EQUIPMENT SECTION
OF CMEC *was screened in detail.*

in the corps and division support areas. When required, they also
provided direct assistance to capturing units. Exploitation functions normally were carried out by these teams at the corps support
area collecting points where they gathered items of intelligence
significance needed to meet requirements of the Combined Materiel
Exploitation Center. Items to be exploited were evacuated to the
center through logistical channels using backhaul transportation
as much as possible. Other equipment was released to the collecting
point commander for disposition in accordance with service
department regulations. Captured enemy materiel requested for
retention by capturing units could be returned by the collecting
point commander after screening and release by personnel at the
center.

The captured material sent to the center was examined and
evaluated to determine enemy materiel threats, technological capabilities, and performance limitations; to produce information from
which military countermeasures were developed; and to provide
continuous input to the national integrated scientific and technical

intelligence program in accordance with Defense Intelligence Agency and Military Assistance Command policy.

In addition to performing exploitation functions at its fixed facility, the Combined Materiel Exploitation Center also maintained "go" teams to provide field exploitation support when required. These quick-reaction teams were airlifted to objective areas to conduct on-site exploitation of large caches of materiel or items of great intelligence significance.

All materiel in the category of communications and electronic equipment was first screened in accordance with Military Assistance Command directives, then evacuated to corps support area collecting points for examination by technical intelligence personnel.

The complete recovery and expeditious evacuation of enemy ammunition and ammunition components contributed essentially to identifying weapons systems used by the Communists and a thorough assessment of the threat posed by each weapons system. Large caches of ammunition and explosives had to be inspected and declared safe for handling by explosive ordnance disposal (EOD) teams before evacuation. Hazardous items were segregated immediately and destroyed by these teams, or by unit ammunition personnel if they were qualified to perform destruction. Explosives and ammunition declared safe for handling were evacuated to the ammunition supply point or ammunition depot designated by the ammunition officer of the capturing command where screening, preliminary exploitation, and selection of items for further evacuation to the Combined Materiel Expoitation Center for detailed examination were conducted. The center co-ordinated preliminary exploitation with the staff explosive ordnance disposal officer at the Military Assistance Command Combat Operations Center to permit technical procedures for safe handling of all first found or newly introduced enemy explosive ordnance to be disseminated promptly throughout the country. All significant items—new, recent, or modified—or enemy material received special handling and were evacuated without delay with captured or recovered technical documents such as gun books, logbooks, packing slips, firing tables, and manuals directly associated with an item of materiel. If the tactical situation did not permit the materiel to be evacuated, a report was forwarded to the Combined Materiel Exploitation Center with a description of the equipment, complete capture data, and other information of value for a technical evaluation of the end item. Photographs of the materiel were highly desirable if the situation permitted.

The Combined Intelligence Center, Vietnam

The Combined Intelligence Center, Vietnam (CICV), was a true product of the combined concept. It became the most sophisticated and capable production facility I have ever known in direct support of wartime operation and planning.

During the early days of the U.S. buildup it was imperative that we be able to produce intelligence as quickly as possible. It was obvious that we would not have time to bring in the necessary units and specialists from the United States; we would have to make do with the meager resources available in Vietnam. This job was assigned to Colonel Frank L. Schaf, Jr., who had previously served as senior adviser to Colonel Ho Van Loi and as such had become thoroughly familiar with the Vietnamese intelligence organization. This experience, coupled with Colonel Schaf's close personal relationship with our counterparts, contributed importantly to the growth of the combined effort.

While the origin of the Combined Intelligence Center cannot be traced to a simple cell, the Target Research and Analysis Center (TRAC) was important in its evolution. The Target Research and Analysis Center had been created in January 1965 to develop targets for Strategic Air Command B–25's that were scheduled to fly missions in support of Military Assistance Command and was housed in a warehouse located on Tan Son Nhut air base. With the increasing emphasis on targeting, the center grew rapidly; by mid-1965 it constituted a significant portion of Military Assistance Command intelligence. More importantly, existing when the decision was reached to develop the Combined Intelligence Center, it had some available space in the warehouse and served as a handy cadre from which to draw specialists to start the U.S. complement for the combined center. Another aspect of its role in the growth of the Combined Intelligence Center was the rapport that had been developed with the Vietnamese in targeting. The Republic of Vietnam Armed Forces intelligence personnel had become accustomed to working with their Military Assistance Command counterparts, and this provided us a foothold that could be expanded into broader combined intelligence production. The targeting function of the Target Research and Analysis Center was assumed by the Targets Branch of the Combined Intelligence Center under Colonel Edward Ratkovich, U.S. Air Force.

From the limited resources available, Colonel Schaf made remarkable progress in developing the U.S. element for the Combined Intelligence Center, which at this stage was a unilateral "joint" enterprise. Drawing heavily from the Target Research and Analysis

Center, the Targets Branch, Support Branch, and Technical Intelligence Branch were fashioned from other elements within the Military Assistance Command intelligence organization. However, there were not enough Americans in Vietnam to man an operation of the scope envisioned, and, though support from the United States would be forthcoming, it would not arrive until late 1965. In mid-August of that year support from the G–2 of U.S. Army, Pacific, was requested. Augmentation personnel from the 319th Military Intelligence Battalion were sought to bolster our over-committed, overworked intelligence force until the units requisitioned from the United States began arriving. During the remainder of August and September 1965, the 319th organized and trained a detachment consisting of an area analysis team, seven order of battle teams, and a detachment headquarters—a total of eleven officers and twenty enlisted men. The detachment closed in Vietnam on 15 October 1965. Colonel Schaf quickly assimilated this welcome addition into the cadre of the expanding Combined Intelligence Center. Because space was at a premium, the area analysis team was housed with the Target Research and Analysis Center in the warehouse at Tan Son Nhut while the order of battle teams had to be located in a building in Cho Lon. In early November 1965 we were informed that the 519th Military Intelligence Battalion, which would provide the personnel for the U.S. complement at the Combined Intelligence Center as well as the combined exploitation centers, had been alerted in August for movement from Fort Bragg, North Carolina, to South Vietnam. Except for a small advance party, the battalion would deploy by ship and would require some forty-five days in transit. This delay necessitated a request through Pacific Command that thirty-two critically needed specialists from the 519th be sent immediately to Vietnam by air; thirty-one of these specialists arrived on 25 November and were assigned to production tasks.

Conditions during these early days were less than ideal. Critical deficiencies in work space, billets, transportation, communications, and mess facilities, complicated by a shortage of men and by long duty hours, presented classic problems in management and leadership. Efficiency suffered because some production elements were located at Cho Lon and some at Tan Son Nhut. In pursuit of more space, we double-decked the warehouse at Tan Son Nhut, but the inconvenience of continuing our production functions while these alterations were in process seriously detracted from our effectiveness. Logistical problems confronted the 519th when it arrived, and difficulties in finding suitable billets as well as administrative area hindered its integration into the Military Assistance Command intelligence organization. But by early December 1965 the warehouse modifications had been completed and the U.S. complement for the proposed combined center was fully operational.

The realization of a combined center as envisioned in my earlier agreement with Colonel Ho Van Loi was still some time away. Not only did the Vietnamese lack the requisite qualified personnel, we did not have a facility suitable for housing a combined operation of the magnitude required. Consequently, plans were drawn up for construction of a new building for the Combined Intelligence Center. Since this was to be joint enterprise and would revert to the Republic of Vietnam Armed Forces upon termination of the U.S. commitment in South Vietnam, the construction was funded as a Military Assistance Program (MAP) project. Completion of the new building became the target date for activation of the Vietnamese complement for the center.

At the end of 1965 the U.S. complement at the Combined Intelligence Center numbered thirty-three men from the 319th Military Intelligence Battalion and 253 permanent party. This number steadily increased as additional elements of the 519th Military Intelligence Battalion arrived; however, we discovered that practically every member of the battalion required either specialized or area training. This added burden had to be placed on the already overtaxed Military Assistance Command intelligence organization and detracted from our capabilities. Despite the inconveniences and difficulties, the 519th soon became operational, and by February 1966 the 319th personnel could be released to return to their parent unit in Hawaii. The Combined Intelligence Center continued to grow and gain in expertise and efficiency. The new building was completed in December 1966, and ribbon-cutting ceremonies marked the official opening on 17 January 1967. The presence of the Vietnamese complement made the occasion particularly significant.

Major Cao Minh Tiep was selected to be the Vietnamese co-director, and this outstanding officer did much to enhance the combined mission accomplishment of the center.

The new center was reputedly the largest fully air-conditioned single-story structure in Southeast Asia. It eventually housed over five hundred U.S. intelligence personnel of all services and more than one hundred Vietnamese intelligence personnel working twenty-four hours a day to provide intelligence support to all combat forces in the Republic of Vietnam.

The organization and functions of the center and its individual branches, once set up and in operation, remained quite stable. Intelligence production requirements were satisfied in order of battle, area analysis, strategic intelligence, technical intelligence, imagery interpretation, trageting, and intelligence data storage. (*Chart 8*)

Again, as in other agreements concerning combined intelligence, U.S. and Vietnamese directors controlled their respective elements of the center. Proximity to one another insured that they could easily discuss matters of mutual concern that affected the operation of the center. Once more, I took care to instill the concept of free and complete exchange of information and total co-operation so that no wall of mistrust and suspicion would be generated. In this combined concept, everything had to be open and sincere.

The Support Branch of the Combined Intelligence Center, charged with personnel administration, supply management, security, and maintenance, accomplished these tasks within its Administrative, Security, and Supply Sections.

CHART 8—ORGANIZATION, COMBINED INTELLIGENCE CENTER, VIETNAM

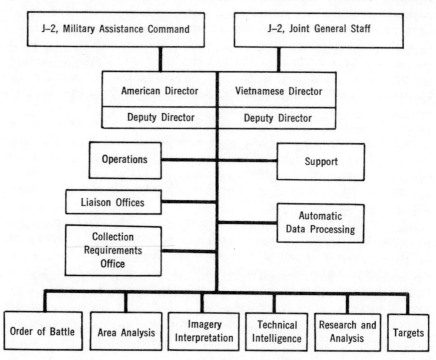

The Operations Branch was responsible for production control, which included editing and dissemination of messages and documents, and was organized with Distribution, Graphics, Editing, and Requirements Sections. In this branch also resided the communications facilities for the center. Eventually, through the use of the J–2 teletype, the center communicated with all major U.S. commanders and senior advisers in Vietnam, thus permitting rapid dissemination of significant intelligence to the combat units in the field—a major goal of the center.

The Automatic Data Processing (ADP) Section automated storage and retrieval of a large portion of the center's data base. The section capably provided analysts and field units with both a narrative printout and a graphic plot of intelligence they required. Although originally designed for support of the Combined Intelligence Center, an equal amount of its work requests were to come from field commanders, both U.S. and Vietnamese. Indeed, many programs were written in Vietnamese. Automatic data processing assistance was as near as the telephone, and, in fact, many units operating near Saigon sent liason officers to the combined center for more personalized contact. If a particular need required immediate response, the center could have information in the hands of a courier within two hours after receipt of a request. The inclusion of Vietnamese military personnel in the Automatic Data Processing Section, trained to operate all of the equipment and working side by side with U.S. specialists, greatly enhanced the intelligence effort. Bilingual printouts were of immediate value to advisers, who could easily co-ordinate and compare information with their counterparts.

In addition to the administrative and management personnel, the headquarters element of the Combined Intelligence Center included liaison officers to communicate personally with other agencies of the country team and with U.S. and other major command intelligence organizations. Also, some people from the collection side were collocated with the producers in the center to insure accurate and timely response by collectors to the needs of the center for additional data or reconnaissance coverage. Colonel Glenn E. Muggelberg in the Intelligence Operations Division understood that this collocation was undertaken in an effort to resolve a recurring problem which cropped up elsewhere in the vast Military Assistance Command organization: though geographically separated, elements in light of their integrated missions must necessarily work in close co-operation with one another. With the problems of inadequate transportation and the scarcity of secure communications that existed in Vietnam at the time, these elements were effectively isolated in their individual compounds. The solution was to put collection directors with the producers in the Combined Intelligence Center.

The Order of Battle Branch (OB Branch) of the Combined Intelligence Center was composed of a headquarters element and three major production elements: Ground Order of Battle (Ground OB), Order of Battle Studies (OB Studies), and Political Order of Battle (Political OB). This branch, which some considered the heart of the center, produced finished intelligence on the eight order of battle factors and on infiltration statistics.

In order to keep its holdings current and complete, the Order of Battle Branch maintained close liaison with other agencies in Saigon (including the other combined intelligence centers), with tactical units in the field, and with the advisers throughout the country. Frequent field trips to compare and exchange information acquainted the corps analysts with the sources of the various types of information available and at the same time familiarized field units with the type of support the Combined Intelligence Center could provide.

The Ground Order of Battle Section had five teams, one for each corps and a Southeast Asia team concerned with North Vietnam, Laos, and Cambodia; these teams were charged with developing military order of battle information on their respective geographical areas. We designed the Order of Battle Studies Section along the lines of the order of battle factors: a strength, composition, and disposition team; a tactics, training, and miscellaneous data team; a combat effectiveness team; and a logistics team. This section produced in-depth, countrywide studies on the enemy's forces.

The Political Order of Battle Section was made up of seven teams organized on the basis of enemy military regions and the Central Office of South Vietnam. The section produced complete and timely intelligence on the boundaries, locations, structure, strengths, personalities, and activities of the Communist political organization, or infrastructure.

A fuller understanding of the functioning of the Order of Battle Branch can be obtained by an examination of the general methodology employed by one of the corps teams of the Ground Order of Battle Section. Information entered the section from a great variety of sources including captured documents, interrogation reports from captives and returnees, agent reports, situation reports, and spot reports. Translations of captured documents and interrogation reports were appreciated, above all, by the analyst, who spent most of his time updating his holdings by evaluating and interpreting these sources. Attention also was given to agent reports, which often provided the initial indication of a change in the composition or disposition of enemy forces. Several thousand reports came into the Combined Intelligence Center each week.

When reports came into the Order of Battle Section, they were scanned for information of immediate intelligence value and then passed for detailed examination to the analyst responsible for the particular unit or area concerned. In the case of a captured document, this procedure may have involved requesting a full translation from the Combined Document Exploitation Center. In the case of an interrogation report, it may have involved levying a specific intelligence collection requirement on the Combined Military Interrogation Center with detailed guidance to assist members of the requirements team and the interrogator in fully exploiting the source for order of battle information. As the analyst developed data, he recorded it in a workbook or on cards for future entry in the computer data base.

Within the analytical process, we were concerned with ascertaining not only the existence of enemy units but also the strength of enemy forces. The corps teams of the Ground Order of Battle Section were charged, therefore, with determining the strength of individual combat and combat support units, a factor revealed principally in captured documents, interrogations, and the analysis of enemy combat losses. The Strength Team of the Order of Battle Studies Section developed countrywide estimates of all categories of strength, including that of guerrillas or militia forces. The corps teams supported the Strength Team by supplying information on specific guerrilla units as well as on combat and combat support units as it became available. The analyst's product thus continually revised and modified the branch's order of battle holdings, which were disseminated to field units, to the Military Assistance Command community, and to Washington through both the *Monthly Order of Battle Summary,* updated daily by cable, and the MACV J–2 Periodic Intelligence Report (PERINTREP), also published monthly.

The Political Order of Battle Section was concerned with the personnel and organization of the Viet Cong infrastructure from hamlet through national level. Information was received in the section from numerous sources: the National Interrogation Center (NIC), the combined exploitation centers, corps and division interrogation center reports, agent reports, rallier or *Hoi Chanh* debriefings, American Embassy reports, intelligence summaries, and special collection program reports. Whatever was extracted was placed in the automated data base, which incorporated both the names of individuals within the infrastructure with their known aliases and, using the international telegraphic code, the diacritical marks that are used with the Vietnamese alphabet and are essential for identification purposes. The section could obtain bilingual printouts that could be sent immediately to the field for use in operations directed against the infrastructure.

The Area Analysis Branch had the mission of supporting operations through the compilation and production of intelligence studies on transportation, communications, and military geography. These included tactical scale studies, area analysis base data studies, a Viet Cong and North Vietnam Army gazetteer, and various other special studies concerned with lines of communication, infiltration routes, avenues of approach, and general terrain analysis. In addition, the branch provided input for the periodic intelligence report and estimates and responded to special requests concerning its area of interest. To accomplish these tasks, the branch functioned with an operations element and five subordinate sections: a lines of communication section with teams responsible for highways, railways, and waterways; an entry zones section with teams responsible for airfields, helicopter landing zones, drop zones, beaches, and ports; a cultural features section with teams for telecommunications, urban areas, and man-made features; a terrain section with teams handling landforms, vegetation, drainage, and soils; a weather section; and, finally, a support element which was responsible for a map and photo library and a reproduction room.

From January to October 1966 the major effort of the Area Analysis Branch was devoted to establishing a data base and the area analysis studies, which were produced at an area scale of 1:250,000 and were referred to as encyclopediae of intelligence because they provided an excellent reference for intelligence information. Each study consisted of three volumes: Book I was a narrative amplifying the overprinted base map which comprised Book II; Book III supplemented Book II with photos and diagrams. Each study covered friendly and enemy operational aspects—lines of communication, cultural features, and weather and climate. Such studies were completed on all areas of South Vietnam, and 1:250,000 map sheets containing intelligence data were reproduced in 400 copies for distribution to customers. Subsequently, to satisfy requirements for this type of intelligence support, we procured cronaflex (a stable base, mylar material) copies of the joint operation graphic series map sheets covering South Vietnam. On the reverse side of each sheet a base map was printed. Intelligence information was then placed on the front of the sheet, and when reproduced on an Ozalid machine, a subdued base map with intelligence superimposed was obtained. Minor changes could be made to the cronaflex sheet without disturbing the base map. Subjects available on cronaflex at a scale of 1:250,000 included cross-country movement, soils, vegetation, geology, and railroads. Originally the plan called for maintaining the data base at this scale, but this proved inadequate for all the information that needed to be plotted. Therefore, the data base was converted to a scale of 1:50,000.

At the same time as the change to 1:50,000 maps, the major emphasis of the Area Analysis Branch shifted to the production of tactical scale studies. The studies were organized into topography, weather, and climate; entry zones; lines of communication; cultural features and telecommunications; cross-country movement; enemy installations; and potential avenues of movement. Except for the first (topography, weather, and climate), which had only a narrative, each study included a narrative and an overprinted map sheet. They were printed in 350 copies to permit wide dissemination. By mid-1967 tactical scale studies had been completed on almost half of South Vietnam, and the remainder were scheduled for completion by November of that year. The studies were to be revised and republished as required.

The Area Analysis Branch constantly sought to improve the quality and timeliness of its products. One step that facilitated speedy response was the acquisition of the cronaflex map sheets. Road, trail, airfield, and landing zone data were posted to the cronaflex masters each day and the branch was thereby enabled to provide in a matter of minutes annotated maps containing the latest intelligence information. This process was used in conjunction with the rapid retrieval possible with the automated system in the Area Analysis Branch. Within a 36-hour period an Ozalid copy of a tactical scale study could be furnished to a requesting unit. A six-map-sheet study required five days for preparation and assembly and fourteen days for printing by the topographic company that supported the Combined Intelligence Center. It was preferable, if time permitted, to have studies printed rather than reproduced by the Ozalid process.

Approximately 60 percent of the Area Analysis Branch's effort was devoted to the maintenance of tactical scale studies; that remaining was occupied by other terrain intelligence requirements such as input to the periodic intelligence report and estimates,

TACTICAL SCALE STUDIES PRODUCED BY THE AREA ANALYSIS BRANCH OF CICV *were used by all Free World forces in planning operations.*

analysis of the effects of the weather on the terrain and enemy capabilities, and the status of routes. Particular attention was paid to requirements for information concerning potential avenues of enemy movement.

Another significant project of the Area Analysis Branch was the preparation of a gazetteer containing 127 1:100,000 Communist map sheets of South Vietnam and reflecting the Viet Cong and North Vietnamese names for places and features. Since the enemy names frequently varied from the South Vietnamese designations, the gazetteer showed the enemy terminology, symbols, and grids with map sheet identification along with the corresponding data that appeared on the U.S. map series. This program was continuous with new names and locales incorporated into the basic document as discovered.

The Technical Intelligence Branch of the Combined Intelligence Center performed equipment analyses, determined weapons and equipment characteristics and specifications, made equipment assessments, and determined vulnerabilities for operational exploitation. In order to produce accurate intelligence on enemy capabilities, vulnerabilities, and order of battle in the technical chemical, ordnance, engineer, quartermaster, medical, signal, and transportation areas, the branch was organized with a headquarters and seven technical specialty sections.

In November 1965 action was initiated to have the 18th Chemical Detachment, 571st Engineer Detachment, 521st Medical Detachment, 528th Ordnance Detachment, 590th Quartermaster Detachment, 18th Signal Detachment, and 30th Transportation Detachment assigned to the 519th Military Intelligence Battalion to support the corresponding sections of the Technical Intelligence Branch. Because these were the only technical intelligence units in Military Assistance Command, centralized control was exercised in order to provide the best possible support for the entire command.

The headquarters element handled the operations and administration of the branch as well as requests for technical intelligence assistance. The Chemical Section monitored the enemy chemical capability, with particular interest in decontamination materials, chemical-related documents, and Soviet-bloc chemical equipment and munitions. The Engineer Section accumulated data on enemy fortifications, structures, tunnel and cave complexes, and barriers about which were produced comprehensive studies of Communist construction, installations, and facilities. The Medical Section was concerned with captured medical supplies and equipment as well as medical examinations of prisoners. The Ordnance Section worked on the exploitation of all items of ordnance equipment, while the Quartermaster Section dealt with enemy uniforms and items of general supply. It also provided information for inclusion in various recognition manuals published by the Combined Intelligence Center. The Signal Section, primarily concerned with Communist communications, was especially interested in signal equipment not of U.S. origin.

In addition to the individual section evaluations and reports, the Technical Intelligence Branch as a unit prepared numerous studies and pamphlets on Communist equipment, arms, and materiel. These studies received wide distribution throughout Vietnam and were valuable in training centers in the United States. One particularly important study receiving a high priority and wide distribution was on the enemy use of mines and booby traps.

Finally, the Technical Intelligence Branch of the Combined Intelligence Center developed and maintained the technical intelligence order of battle and provided current information on all of the technical service or support-type units. This information was

AMERICAN AND VIETNAMESE INTELLIGENCE SPECIALISTS *examine a captured enemy rocket launcher.*

published in studies designed to give the customer as much information as possible about the enemy's capabilities and vulnerabilities in the technical service fields. The first such study, *NVA/VC Signal Order of Battle,* was published during January 1967.

In the Imagery Interpretation (II) Branch of the Combined Intelligence Center, readouts were made of all types of imagery—photo, infrared, and side-looking airborne radar—and furnished to the other branches of the center that required it. The Imagery Interpretation Branch had two sections. The Operations Section was organized along geographical lines with a team for each of the Vietnamese corps as well as out-of-country teams; the Support Section included a film library, a maintenance team, and a photography laboratory. The air-conditioned laboratory, constructed in mid-1967, provided specialized photographic processing support to all branches within the center. Naturally, we attempted to provide the Imagery Interpretation Branch with the most advanced and best equipment available in its field.

A survey team from the Office of the Assistant Chief of Staff for Intelligence at Department of the Army and the Automatic Data Field Systems Command in December 1965 came to Saigon on my request. They recommended that we procure certain equipment for the proposed combined center. Their research indicated that the center would need equipment which could accelerate the extraction, analysis, and dissemination of intelligence from aerial imagery. We initiated Project Concrete to secure the needed equipment and submitted requisitions on 13 December 1965. The first shipment of Project Concrete imagery interpretation equipment arrived on 15 December 1966 and consisted of twelve simple roll-film light tables to be used with zoom optics, two AR 85 Viewer-Computers, three Itek rear-projection viewers, and a CAF Model 910 Ozalid printmaster. The second shipment arrived on 14 January 1967 and included four AR 85 Viewer-Computers, one Map-O-Graph, three Itek variable-width viewers, a microdensitometer with clean-room module, and one photo rectifier. The final shipment came late in February 1967 and included six multisensor take-up tables with a supply of replacement parts.

The AR 85 Viewer-Computer was designed to perform rapid and accurate mensuration on all types of imagery—infrared, radar, and photography, including panoramic photographs. Some of the more important functions performed by the computer included determination of true ground position expressed either in geographic or universal transverse mercator co-ordinates, determination of height, area measurement, and measurement of straight or curvilinear distances. A typical project on which these machines were employed was the analysis of rice production in the IV Corps Tactical Zone.

The Itek variable-width viewer stood as one of the most important items of equipment in the inventory of the Imagery Interpretation Branch. The viewer was used initially to scan the duplicate positive or duplicate negative imagery received at the Combined Intelligence Center. Through a rear-view process, the image was projected onto a large viewing screen. The operator, seated in front of the viewer, was able to have the imagery move at whatever speed he desired. When he detected something of significance, he could opt to enlarge the projected image three, twelve, or thirty times, a feature which in itself added a new dimension to the imagery interpretation process at the center. For example, the optimum altitude for high panoramic reconnaissance missions was 15,000 feet. This resulted in a photo scale of 1:15,000, too small for tactical interpretation. Using the variable-width viewer, the scale could be increased to 1:500 at 30 times magnification without appreciable loss of resolution. One of the viewers, equipped with a printer attachment, produced an 18x24-inch photograph of the image projected on the screen within approximately forty seconds. One such photograph of a camouflaged surface-to-air missile site in North Vietnam, made from film taken a short while earlier, was used to brief U.S. Air Force strike pilots in Saigon. The pilots returned and destroyed the site, which had been located by an imagery interpreter using the Itek viewer.

A closer look at some of the representative projects of the Imagery Interpretation Branch will give a better understanding of its operation and the use of its equipment. One important project, the Photo Study Program, originated in December 1966 when the III Corps Tactical Zone imagery interpretation team was directed to make a photo study of the Lo Go area in Tay Ninh Province. This study was intended to furnish photo intelligence on an area in which elements of the Central Office of South Vietnam reportedly had been operating. Imagery interpreters first made a detailed analysis of photography of the area to identify and annotate all items of military significance. Then, in order to determine the arrangement and interrelationship of the defensive positions, trails, and other military activity discovered on the individual photos, mosaics were constructed. In the mosaics the information noted on the individual photos began to form a pattern, particularly highlighting the lines of communication and area defenses. Instead

IMAGERY INTERPRETER *removes photocopy produced by the Itek variable-width viewer with printer.*

of a trail simply crossing one photograph, it could be followed over a large area to aid in the identification of entire defensive systems. Because this study resulted in some twenty mosaics, an indexing system had to be devised that would allow the user to locate a particular mosaic without going through the whole set. To do this, the traces of the mosaics were plotted on 1:50,000 maps and were numbered. Overlays were prepared, also at a scale of 1:50,000, showing what intelligence items were found on each mosaic that indicated lines of communication and defensive positions. Thus the completed photo study packet contained defense and lines of communications overlays, a 1:50,000 index to the mosaics, and the annotated mosaics. However, it was apparent that the full value of the studies could not be realized unless the packet could be reproduced in sufficient quantity and in a convenient format to permit its use by each unit in the area covered by the study. The original size of the complete packet—30x40 inches—was too large for field use. To overcome this difficulty, arrangements were made with the U.S. Air Force 13th Reconnaissance Technical Squadron to have the packet reproduced at a 50 percent reduction of the original size and in a quantity to satisfy all requesters. The popularity and success of the Photo Study Program in III Corps led to its adoption as a project for all the corps imagery interpretation teams in the Combined Intelligence Center. By May 1967, sixty-four photo studies had been produced.

Practical applications for these studies were almost limitless. Special Forces units used them in setting up security for the Civilian Irregular Defense Group camps and hamlets, and advisers used them for briefing and debriefing their counterparts and troops. They were utilized similarly in briefing and debriefing agents and were of great value in the planning and conduct of U.S. and South Vietnamese ground operations. In many cases individual mosaics were removed from the packet and distributed down to platoon level to supplement maps and to provide intelligence on the platoon tactical area of responsibility. In addition to field applications, the photo studies were valued by the targeting and strike objectives teams of the Targets Branch of the Combined Intelligence Center in determining targets for B–52 strikes and tactical unit objectives. In many cases the studies were used for comparison with new photographs to detect evidence or indications of recent enemy activity.

Starting from the receipt of the photography, fourteen days were required to complete and reproduce a study. Because of the increased demand, the Imagery Interpretation Branch decided that all original mosaics and the negatives made during the reproduction process would be held in a repository at the Combined Intelligence Center, where they were indexed and filed for easy retrieval. Subsequent requirements for any single mosaic could be filled in a matter of hours.

The Research and Analysis Branch of the Combined Intelligence Center developed intelligence and produced reports and studies on the economic, political, sociological, and psychological characteristics and vulnerabilities of the enemy's military and political forces. The branch was organized into a South Vietnam section and a Southeast Asia section that was concerned with enemy activities in Laos, Cambodia, and North Vietnam as well as with information concerning Communist Chinese involvement in the war or war effort. Strategic studies produced covered such topics as Viet Cong taxation, soldiers' morale, the effectiveness of B–52 strikes and herbicide operations, and characteristics of the North Vietnamese Army soldiers fighting in South Vietnam. (*Appendix G*) A typical study was compiled from more than six hundred enemy documents, interrogation reports, and field intelligence reports. The branch also provided intelligence support for psychological warfare operations by passing to psychological operations personnel a summary of all information applicable to that field. Analyses and comments on trends noted in Communist psychological operations also were prepared. Receiving input from all other activities of the Combined Intelligence Center, the Targets Branch was responsible for compiling the necessary intelligence to develop targets for exploitation by combat forces available to General Westmoreland. Basically, the Targets Branch was charged with locating the enemy, an intriguing and challenging task.

The pattern analysis technique began with the development of an extensive data base consisting of all available information regarding enemy activities in a particular area. The data base included every instance of enemy activity contained in intelligence files, for example ambush sites used by the Viet Minh during the war with France. Criteria for inclusion in the data base were continually revised, but as many as thirty-five factors were sometimes considered. Typical of information put into the data base were:

1. Reported locations and movements of Communist units
2. All agent reports of enemy activity
3. All contacts and incidents
4. Known and suspected installations
5. Reports of logistical operations or activities
6. Infiltration routes
7. Friendly units and operations, including Arc Light strikes, secondary explosions, and imagery interpretation reports

These data were posted on transparent overlays on 1:250,000 maps. The overlays were kept current and constituted the pattern analysis files. Overlays were prepared by subject; that is, a separate overlay was made for logistical activities, another for contacts and incidents. Patterns were detected or identified by a detailed examination of each overlay by subject. Next, overlays were combined, as many as five at a time, and placed simultaneously over the map. The objective was to determine if there were any apparent or possible relationship between the different subject activities. For example, did logistical activities posted on the logistics overlay seem to support the combat operations posted on the contact and incident overlay? Certain standardizations of format as well as innovations by individual analysts contributed to the effectiveness of the comparisons and the determination of patterns.

In order that the analytical process yield patterns from which the enemy and his habits could be identified and targets formed, the analysts concurrently studied subject indicators such as those in the following hypothetical situation:

1. *Terrain considerations (obtained from base map)*. For the enemy to operate, suitable water, trail, and road transportation had to be available. These modes of travel and communication connected the logistical bases with infiltration embarkation points, other bases, and nearby unit operational areas.

2. *Reported locations and contacts (plotted on overlay)*. A concentration of reported and accepted enemy unit sightings, in areas of firm enemy control where friendly agent penetration was difficult, indicated the existence of a supply or retraining center, possibly a base area itself.

3. *Confirmed unit movement (plotted on overlay)*. The analysis of identified unit movements in conjunction with installations, incidents, and agent reports aided in establishing operational areas, command procedures, unit missions and objectives, and methods of operation. Comparison of unit movement with known trails determined from aerial photography suggested enemy lines of communication.

4. *Unit sightings (plotted on overlay)*. Unit sightings were analyzed in relation to friendly and enemy installations. They represented densities of reported enemy activity which, besides identifying specific enemy organizations, could assist in locating enemy operational areas. Conversely, an absence of unit sightings may have stemmed from insufficient friendly ground surveillance and agent nets as well as from an absence of enemy activity.

5. *Incidents (plotted on overlay)*. Incidents could be analyzed, either by type or in total, to establish enemy objectives and methods of engagement. A relative lack of terrorism, sabotage, harassment, or propaganda activity in a populated area where government authority was tenuous suggested a high degree of enemy control over the population, an entrenchment which might have meant a base for his operations. On the other hand, a high level of such activity, nestled against the perimeter of a low incident area, may have indicated an effort by the enemy to expand or maintain a protective buffer around a base.

6. *Installations (plotted on overlay).* Types of logistical installations were examined as they related to the terrain and to each other, and they could be analyzed in relation to confirmed and reported unit movement. Generally, we attempted to prove the validity of the reported enemy installations, to establish characteristics in their development, and to determine their relative importance to individual or combined units. A high density of food, ordnance, and medical installations, storage caches, or training sites usually defined a base area.

7. *Friendly operations and order of battle (plotted on overlay).* Consideration had to be extended to friendly forces, since their presence influenced the normal pattern of enemy activity such as unit movement, installations, base areas, and operational procedures. Friendly installations, often not only barriers but also targets, needed to be studied to reveal enemy operational techniques and methods of movement.

8. *B–52 strikes (plotted on overlay).* The B–52 program's effectiveness could be partially evaluated by comparison with enemy installations, unit movement, and sightings. The status of enemy installations could be examined, and enemy techniques of countering air strikes might be revealed, by comparing the time relationships between reports of installations and unit movements and the corresponding strike.

9. *Imagery interpretation readout (plotted on overlay).* Intelligence gained from various forms of imagery provided a means of checking other reports and often produced added detailed information on a specific area of interest. All enemy activities thus needed to be examined collaterally with imagery of the particular area. Photos provided confirmation of enemy installations, lines of communication, and operational zones. Side-looking airborne radar, for instance, usefully detected night movements of watercraft.

In the final phase of pattern analysis, the over-all evaluation, the analysts synthesized the separate trends developed during the analysis phase. Such a process measured the relative probability of an existing element, activity, or characteristic, based on logical relationships and hypotheses developed by analysis.

The pattern analysis technique could have been just one of many designed to assist in intelligence production and should be kept in mind as a format serving to hold and exploit a potential reservoir of information. The process was a continuous one in which all phases were developing simultaneously. By no means did we explore all methods of analysis, but our program assisted in achieving economy of force by focusing intelligence and operational resources on areas where the enemy was most likely to be located and helped avoid wasting resources elsewhere. In this manner we accurately located enemy base areas.

Finished intelligence prepared through the use of the pattern analysis technique was disseminated according to existing priorities. Feedback from the using units, consisting of after action reports or other field reports, provided data necessary to confirm or refine methods of analysis. Along this line, field reports helped to determine the validity of the sources and information used during analysis and aided in the continuing evaluation of the intelligence that was produced.

The geographical organization of many of the subelements within the Combined Intelligence Center permitted the pooling of specialists from the various branches to provide concentration on a specific area of interest such as one of the four Vietnamese corps tactical zones or the enemy sanctuaries of Laos, Cambodia, and North Vietnam. At the center itself, the order of battle analysts, imagery interpreters, targets personnel, and area analysts worked together on their respective corps geographic regions to detect those areas which would become of primary interest to the tactical commands.

General Westmoreland directed that senior field commanders and selected members of their staffs visit the Combined Intelligence Center to become acquainted with its capabilities. These visits showed that in-depth analysis and close co-operation with the Vietnamese were the main strengths of the center. As in any good partnership, both parties benefited. The Vietnamese profited from American material resources, technical knowledge, and experience, while the United States capitalized on the knowledge which the Vietnamese possessed about the enemy and the area of operations and the continuity which resulted from the long-term assignments of the Vietnamese specialists to intelligence production.

The Sector Intelligence Support Program

One of the fundamental elements of the intelligence organization in Vietnam was the advisory system. Before the U.S. buildup, the advisers stationed throughout the country provided a large portion of the intelligence information received by J–2, Military Assistance Command. They were the most responsive of the resources available to the intelligence staff, even though remote locations, primitive communications, and limited transportation detracted from the timeliness of their reports. With the escalation of the U.S. role, it was evident that the advisers would continue to be very important to the success of our intelligence effort. They were our best contact with the people of Vietnam, and in a counterinsurgency, access to the populace is essential. Their capacities could be improved particularly in the areas of collection, processing, and reporting at the sector and subsector level. In addition, the combined intelligence concept needed to be extended to the advisers. The identification and elimination of the Communist infrastructure would depend in large measure upon sector- and subsector-level intelligence.

Capabilities and vulnerabilities of the Viet Cong infrastructure, or, as I called it, the Viet Cong political order of battle, were as much a part of the enemy war-making potential as was his military order of battle. In July 1965 Colonel Loi and I published a two-inch-thick memeographed report titled "Viet Cong Political Order of Battle." This report showed us what we needed and what we had. We had a long way to go, but we knew what we had to do.

A political order of battle branch was part of the original organization of the Combined Intelligence Center. Data to support this program were automated very early. A special combined collection plan was prepared and implemented to focus maximum efforts to collect information at the sector and subsector level. The number of advisers at sector and subsector was increased. However, co-operation and co-ordination among intelligence agencies in sectors left much to be desired. I embarked on a program to correct this deficiency.

First, my staff wrote a sector intelligence guide. This guide was a comprehensive handbook that not only described, step by step, how the sector intelligence adviser accomplished his mission, but also served to explain to all commanders and staff officers in Vietnam how the sector intelligence program worked and what it could do. The guide was carefully prepared and fully staffed. The U.S. Embassy, the Military Assistance Command, and the Joint General Staff approved it. The guide was issued in English and Vietnamese. Colonel Loi and I wanted to be sure that key people not only received the guide but also understood it and implemented it, so we created the Combined Intelligence School. We selected the Vietnamese and U.S. instructors; we approved the curriculum and attended the dress rehearsal of all lessons. The course lasted four days. All Vietnamese sector S–2's and their U.S. advisers, representatives from ten sectors at a time, attended the school together. The students not only studied all aspects of sector intelligence but also received a comprehensive review of pertinent Military Assistance Command and Republic of Vietnam Armed Forces intelligence directives. The students visited all the combined centers and learned what the centers could do to help them and that the centers would accept their requests by telephone. The initial instruction was aimed at the sector S–2's and their U.S. counterparts, but the ultimate goal was to have all major commanders, key advisers, and intelligence officers attend the school. Classroom presentation utilized two instructors, one an American who spoke English and the other a Vietnamese who taught in his native language. Provided earphones, students heard a simultaneous translation of each presentation. Even the charts were bilingual. The inaugural class, made up of the sector S–2's and U.S. advisers from the ten most critical provinces in South Vietnam, was personally welcomed by Colonel Loi and myself. We each addressed the students on this occasion to demonstrate our concern for instruction of this nature.

Upon completing the course the students were fully familiar with the intricacies of combined intelligence and, more importantly, were well versed in the sector intelligence program which included comprehensive coverage of the Communist infrastructure. Returning to their posts, these officers better appreciated what their intelligence staffs could do. In addition to the direct benefits resulting from the instruction, the school provided an example of what U.S.–Vietnamese co-operation could accomplish. Frequently it provided the first exposure for the students to a sophisticated combined operation and did much to set the example for working together.

I always made it a point to have the young U.S. officer advisers to my billet for dinner. From these evening sessions I gained a greater appreciation of the difficulties they faced in the field. It is too easy for a commander to be isolated by the bureaucracy of a headquarters.

As commander of the sector military intelligence detachment, the sector intelligence adviser had the mission to provide and supervise U.S. intelligence personnel required to support the intelligence advisory effort and operations within each sector; to advise and assist Vietnamese counterparts while working with them; and to direct the over-all U.S. military intelligence effort of all subsectors within the sector. He also had to collate and disseminate all collected information regarding the maintenance of security to subsector and adjacent sectors; monitor, co-ordinate, and support U.S., South Vietnamese, and Free World Military Assistance Forces intelligence activities within each sector area of responsibility, with particular emphasis on collection of infrastructure and order of battle data; co-ordinate with appropriate U.S., South Vietnamese, and Free World Military Assistance Forces and agencies, as well as U.S. advisers, to facilitate timely lateral and vertical transmittal of information; and establish, develop, and participate in U.S., South Vietnamese, and Free World Military Assistance Forces intelligence activities as required.

The sector intelligence adviser made recommendations on intelligence objectives of operations within his sector and advised on the proper utilization of the Vietnamese Regional Forces intelligence platoon attached to each sector S–2. His efforts and accomplishments and those of his detachment were founded in the concept of combined intelligence operations with his Vietnamese counterparts. The extent that he worked in combination with his counterpart determined the degree of success he achieved. It was, therefore, a prime criterion of the Sector Intelligence Support Program that it contribute to this working relationship.

To support this relationship, I placed additional emphasis on support functions already established. Additional responsibilities for support to be provided by the Military Assistance Command J-2 to the sector intelligence adviser were levied. These fell within the broad areas of order of battle information, maps and charts, photographic coverage, studies and estimates, personnel, sector intelligence guide, staff visits, and training and orientation. A number of projects were established that supported specific sector requirements. Seven of these are of particular interest:

1. Additional distribution was made of sets of bilingual vocabulary cards pertaining to seven specific areas of intelligence. These areas included the intelligence adviser, counterintelligence, target presentation, imagery interpretation, intelligence planning, order of battle, and intelligence collection. These cards helped to communicate exact meanings of words and terms and to assure understanding between the sector intelligence adviser and his counterpart.

2. Map information brochures covering individual sectors were forwarded to each of the forty-four sector intelligence advisers. The brochures contained updated map indexes, notes on current status and availability, plus single copies of all current maps of the sector. The objective was to provide each sector intelligence adviser an indexed map library.

3. The Combined Intelligence Center, Vietnam, was equipped with computers which stored the intelligence data base and produced printouts from automated files on enemy ground order of battle, special agent reports, imagery interpretation, military biog-

raphies, enemy installations, helicopter landing zones, logistical movement, railroad bridges, enemy movement, highway bridges, road reports, inland waterways, airfields, Arc Light incidents, infiltration, tax collection points, letter box numbers, drop zones, beaches, and political biographies. Studies and reports of specific interest to the sector intelligence detachment which utilized this retrieval system were base data studies, photo package studies, and order of battle reports and studies.

Through the base data studies program extensive information on area analysis subjects was provided. These studies were made for the entire Republic of Vietnam on a scale of 1:250,000 and could be obtained through normal map supply channels. Area analysis information was provided at a tactical scale for specific areas of high interest through the war zone studies program. Sector intelligence advisers could nominate specific areas for inclusion in this program.

A photo package studies program was initiated through which the sector intelligence adviser was provided with a comprehensive photographic package covering significant area within his sector.

4. The monthly order of battle summary provided recapitulation and breakdown of enemy units and strengths by categories of acceptance and corps tactical zones, maps of corps zones with units indicated, organizational structures, loss statistics, newly reported units, and infiltration statistics. Order of battle reports and studies provided technical data on enemy organizational structure, rear services, combat support arms, training, and infiltration. In addition, collected data in the Combined Intelligence Center order of battle files was provided on request.

5. In addition to routine staff visits conducted by members of J–2, Military Assistance Command, the sector intelligence visitation program was initiated with the appointment of a deputy for sector intelligence. This appointment focused responsibility for monitoring the entire sector program and provided me with an accurate assessment of the effectiveness of sector operations.

6. A sector intelligence guide was distributed to the field. This guide was a current reference to sector intelligence organization, functions, and relationships. Although directed specifically at the sector level, it was intended to assist the intelligence effort at all levels. Provisions were made for the frequent update of this publication, and it was co-ordinated with the U.S. Embassy, Saigon, and J–2, Joint General Staff.

7. A combined intelligence school was set up for the Republic of Vietnam Armed Forces sector intelligence officers and their

advisers. The scope of the intelligence subjects covered was quite broad and ranged from "Handling POW's" to "VC/NVA Base Area Study Techniques." All training aids were displayed in both Vietnamese and English, and at the time of the instructor's presentation a translated version was given by means of a closed communication system. Ten Vietnamese and ten U.S. officers attended each four-day session. The nitial class was conducted 10–13 January 1967, and the eighth class terminated on 28 April, resulting in a total of 150 Vietnamese and U.S. officers representing all forty-four sectors having attended. The next class was scheduled for 16 May 1967.

In order to place emphasis on all of the above activities I created the position of Deputy for Sector Intelligence and assigned Colonel Stone W. Quillian, U.S. Marine Corps, to that job. He reported directly to me at least once a week. The remainder of the time he was visiting the forty-four sectors to determine how the program was working. His goal also involved improving the promptness and completeness of our reporting system. While this procedure seemed rather fundamental, complications surfaced. At sector level, intelligence operations were more a police function than a military one, and lateral exchange of information was not what it should have been. The emphasis on offensive operations overtaxed the advisers, who were expected to provide timely, accurate, and complete combat intelligence to the local commander while at the same time serving as the keystone of the Military Assistance Command collection effort directed at the enemy political apparatus. The situation was ameliorated by the assignment of trained military intelligence officers as full-time sector intelligence advisers and the deployment of three-man intelligence teams (later increased to seven men) to the sectors.

Indigenous intelligence resources of the South Vietnamese Army sector S–2 varied greatly between provinces but normally included a Regional Forces and Popular Forces intelligence platoon. Working closely with their counterparts, the advisory teams launched elaborate programs incorporating agent nets and informant systems with combat and reconnaissance patrols. As the national intelligence system became more sophisticated, the quality of the sector-level product showed marked improvement. (*Appendix H*) Source control procedures, better collection management, and efficient fiscal accountability contributed to better productivity. Early attempts to develop a good collection program were hindered by the shortage of men experienced in the intracacies of such operations; however, this situation was eventually corrected by the assignment of an intelligence specialist to each sector headquarters. The information gathered by the sector apparatus was disseminated through U.S. and Vietnamese channels to higher, lower, and adjacent commands. (*Chart 9*)

At this point it is prudent to explain the role of the Province Intelligence Coordination Committees (PICC's), which were not a part of the Sector Intelligence Program. These committees had been established by national decree in November 1964 to serve as the senior intelligence agency within each province. In consonance with the province chief's over-all responsibility of government, the committee functioned as a supervisory body to direct and monitor all intelligence activities within the province and was charged with guiding, supervising, and co-ordinating the operations of both military and civilian agencies; receiving, collating, and disseminating intelligence gathered by the province units; maintaining a centralized provincial source registry; and advising the province chief on the enemy situation as well as on friendly intelligence activities. The committee had great potential, but as Colonel Quillian discovered during his visits through the country, the standard of performance and effectiveness varied widely. In fact, some of the committees existed only on paper and the U.S.–South Vietnamese sector intelligence team assumed, in many instances,

CHART 9—SECTOR COMBINED INTELLIGENCE OPERATIONS

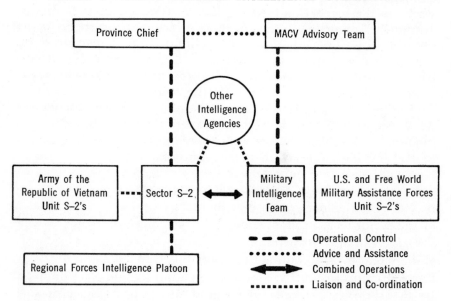

complete responsibility for all important functions of the committee. The sector S–2 was not a member of the committee, but he and his U.S. adviser often were invited to attend meetings and many were very active in its affairs.

From its inception the Sector Intelligence Program experienced difficulties with communication. The absence of a secure country-wide intelligence transmission system hindered the submission of timely reports and precluded real-time responses to requirements from higher headquarters. There were instances where intelligence reports sent by mail from I Corps reached Saigon faster than those electrically transmitted. Eventually, secure communications were established between Saigon and each corps headquarters, but, still, messages to sector and below had to be relayed. Hard-copy reports were the most common means of communications for sector personnel.

Another problem affecting sector intelligence concerned availability of adequate interrogation facilities. Although local agreements enabled sector personnel to obtain the intelligence reports resulting from police interrogations, the failure to obtain space for the military in the sector police interrogation centers, upon which we had depended, caused delay in the exploitation of prisoners and detainees.

In most sectors noticeable improvements were evident. Reporting on enemy irregular forces and infrastructure improved, but the Office of Special Assistant to the Ambassador, without co-ordination with Military Assistance Command, took over control of the files on the infrastructure located at the sectors. I could not believe such a report until I visited a sector and was refused permission to see the infrastructure file by a member of the embassy. Without unity of command such things happen. This was one of several indications to me that in spite of all our efforts things were not going so well as they should. I visited the embassy and was assured that the situation would be corrected. Not long thereafter, I left Vietnam.

The Combined Intelligence Staff

The Combined Intelligence Staff (CIS) came into existence on 18 November 1966, but its actual genesis goes back to the spring and early summer of that year. At that time, with the government of Vietnam embroiled in an internal political crisis, the security situation in and around Saigon had steadily deteriorated. I directed an intensive collection campaign against Viet Cong Military Region IV (which included Saigon) with the objective of alerting the U.S.

as well as the South Vietnamese authorities on this growing threat. Resulting intelligence proved that Saigon was a priority target of the enemy. After I briefed General Westmoreland and the U.S. Mission Council I was asked to meet with U.S. Deputy Ambassador Koren to discuss actions that could be taken. I submitted a plan that was approved in principle by the MACV command and Ambassador Koren. In September I met with Brigadier General Nguyen Ngoc Loan, director general of the Vietnamese National Police and director of the Military Security Service (MSS) of the Republic of Vietnam Armed Forces, to discuss the plan. I briefed General Loan on the plan and left it with him to study. A combined intelligence staff was envisioned, with mission of producing intelligence on the identification and location of Viet Cong operating in Military Region IV (which corresponds to Gia Dinh and the southern half of Dau Nghia and Binh Tong Provinces) and of disseminating this intelligence to user agencies for apprehension and exploitation of enemy personnel.

This concept was approved in November by Prime Minister Nguyen Cao Ky, the Vietnamese Joint General Staff, and the U.S. Mission Council. In addition to the Combined Intelligence Staff, Operation FAIRFAX/RANG DONG, consisting of three U.S. and three Army of the Republic of Vietnam battalions, was initiated on 1 December 1966 with the mission of searching out and destroying the Viet Cong main force units, guerrillas, and infrastructure in the Military Region IV area. Operation FAIRFAX/RANG DONG and the Combined Intelligence Staff were to be the primary elements of Campaign Cong Tac 4 (Vietnamese for mission), aimed at the elimination of Military Region IV.

The initial actions of the Combined Intelligence Staff were to compile a blacklist of Military Region IV infrastructure personalities in support of the combined U.S. and Vietnamese military actions within this area. The staff compiled over three thousand names and assorted personality data during this period and provided them to the U.S. and Vietnamese units. These data were acquired by the area coverage desk teams, which visited all district headquarters and intelligence agencies and reviewed their files, extracting pertinent data. The result was a central registry or data base of known Viet Cong in Military Region IV. This registry was laboriously assembled by hand, the only method available at that time. After this initial phase, a more systematic and sophisticated method greatly improved and facilitated the work of the staff.

The Combined Intelligence Staff was placed under the operational control of General Loan. Vietnamese assigned to the staff represented the Military Security Service; National Police; Central Intelligence Organization (CIO), Republic of Vietnam; J–2, Joint General Staff, Republic of Vietnam Armed Forces; and G–2, Capital Military District (CMD). On the U.S. side, J – 2, Military Assistance Command; the Office of the Special Assistant of the U.S. Embassy; and the 135th and 149th Military Intelligence Groups provided men and support. The Combined Intelligence Staff consisted of fifteen U.S. and fifty Vietnamese personnel. (*Chart 10*) The directorate consisted of three individuals, a Military Security Service major who acted as chief, and two U.S. deputies, a Military Assistance Command J–2 lieutenant colonel and a civilian representative from the Office of the Special Assistant. The operations office also consisted of three individuals who were nominally the three assistants to the members of the directorate (a Vietnamese National Police official, a Military Assistance Command J–2 major, and a representative from the Office of the Special Assistant) and who functioned as chiefs of the Administrative and

CHART 10—FLOW CHART, COMBINED INTELLIGENCE STAFF

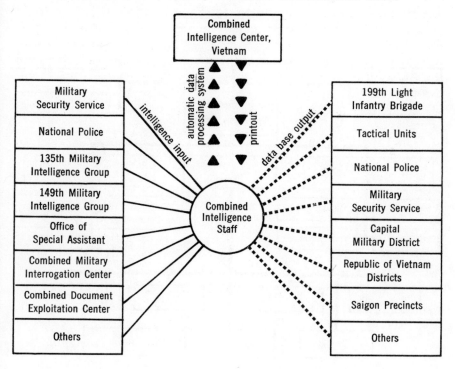

Support Area Coverage and Analysis and Dissemination Branches, respectively. Special representatives, Vietnamese officers, represented the Military Security Service; Central Intelligence Organization; J–2, Joint General Staff; and G–2, Capital Military District, and acted as points of contact with these agencies. The Combined Intelligence Staff had operational control of a field search unit and a screening section (*Chart 11*).

The systematic identification and location of Viet Cong and the rapid retrieval of these data in usable form was made possible by the use of the automatic data processing system located at the Combined Intelligence Center, Vietnam. (*Chart 12*) Data in the form of intelligence information reports, interrogation reports, and captured documents were analyzed by the U.S. and Vietnamese desk officer teams. Personality data on Viet Cong were then extracted from these reports and transposed on IBM worksheets in the following categories:

CHART 11—ORGANIZATION, COMBINED INTELLIGENCE STAFF

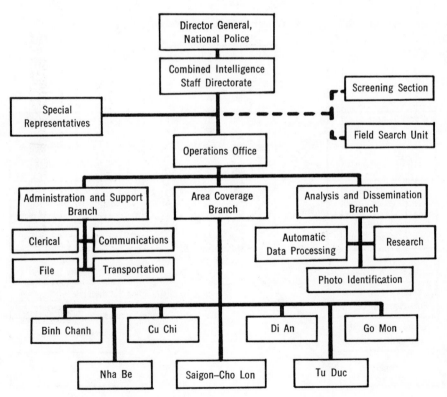

CHART 12—DATA BASE INPUT (CICV)

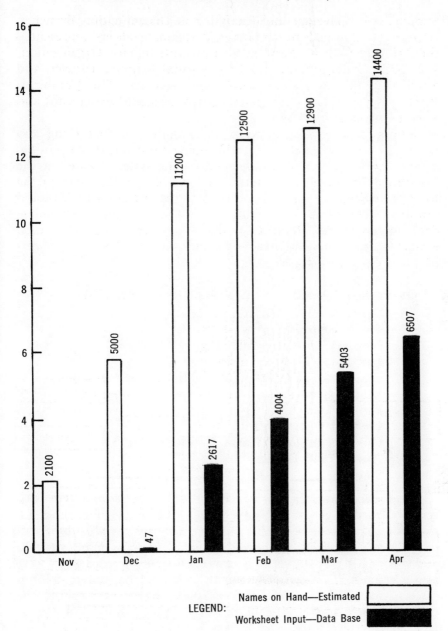

LEGEND:
Names on Hand—Estimated
Worksheet Input—Data Base

Elements of Information for Data Base

I.   Serial Number
   A.   Province
   B.   District
   C.   Number of Input

II. Date of Information

III. Universal Transverse Mercator Co-ordinates

IV. Source
   A.   Unit
   B.   Type
   C.   Number

V.   Personal Data
   A.   Names
   B.   Date and Place of Birth
   C.   Titles
   D.   Organization
   E.   Operational Location
   F.   Party Membership
   G.   North Vietnamese Affiliation
   H.   Residence, Past and Present
   I.   Education and Occupation, Military and Civilian
   J.   Ethnic Group
   K.   Family Data
   L.   Physical Characteristics
   M.   Government of Vietnam Connections
   N.   Awards and Decorations
   O.   Status

The serial number block contained a number and letter designation for the geographic area as well as a sequence number for the individual identified. This number was used for all subsequent worksheets submitted on the individual. The date of information and the location by universal transverse mercator co-ordinates were also extracted, if known. The fourth category, the source of information, included the U.S. or Vietnamese agency furnishing the report as well as the type of report and log or file number to facilitate retrieval of the basic data.

The most important category of the information programmed into the data base was personal data on the individual. The true name was spelled out in English, followed by a phonetic spelling in the Vietnamese telegraphic code, which simulates, in letter form, the diacritical markings of the Viet Cong language. Any cover names or aliases were also shown, although in this case the telegraphic code was not used. The rest of the personal data category contained any information available on the individual's position in the Viet Cong organization, geographic, location, Communist party and North Vietnamese affiliation, educational and occupational skills, family data, and physical characteristics. The final item, status, indicated whether the individual had been captured or was still at large.

As of 30 April 1967, the Combined Intelligence Staff had introduced 6,507 names into the data base and was averaging over 1,200 names per month.

An important function of the Combined Intelligence Staff was the direct support furnished to the U.S. and South Vietnamese units operating in the Military Region IV area. A field search unit, consisting of three 49-man Police Field Force platoons, accompanied the U.S. and Vietnamese units conducting cordon and search operations in Military Region IV. After the military unit had cordoned off the area, the police entered the hamlet, checking the identification cards of all inhabitants as well as making a complete search of the area for tunnels, personnel, weapons, and supplies. A representative of the Combined Intelligence Staff accompanied the unit on these operations and provided photographs of Viet Cong as well as the blacklists for the district concerned. These blacklists were used in the search of the hamlet as an aid in apprehension. Suspects were taken to a screening center which was also under the operational control of the Combined Intelligence Staff. There suspects were interrogated, photographed, and fingerprinted. Those found to be offenders were arrested, and the remainder were released.

In addition to Operation FAIRFAX, the Combined Intelligence Staff in January 1967 provided support for Operation CEDAR FALLS, the U.S. and South Vietnamese multidivision search and clear operation which was highly successful against Military Region IV.

Activities of the staff reached a high point in May and June 1967, when it conducted a co-ordinated operation with the Capital Military District, the Combined Security Committee, components of the National Police, and Operation FAIRFAX. A tight security cordon was placed around Saigon and resulted in the arrest of seventy-three confirmed Communist clandestine action agents and sappers. From the inception of the Combined Intelligence Staff until 1 December 1967, approximately five hundred Viet Cong action agents were apprehended in Saigon and environs. The significance of these arrests—and the success of the staff—cannot be fully measured but unquestionably contributed to the Communist failures in Saigon during the 1968 *Tet* offensive.

In May 1967, I published a report on the Combined Intelligence Staff. In the preface to that report I wrote:

The purpose of this FACT BOOK is to present the mission, history, functions, and capabilities of the Combined Intelligence Staff (CIS), the most recent and certainly a unique addition to the family of Combined Centers established by J2, MACV, in coordination with the Republic of Vietnam Armed Forces and the Government of Vietnam.

This staff was conceived and created as a prototype counterintelligence organization, designed to collate, analyze, and disseminate intelligence on Viet Cong Military Region 4—the area surrounding and including Saigon.

The CIS, as a pilot program, has made remarkable progress in the short period of its existence. Its recent venture into the operational field, viewed with some misgivings at first, has paid off handsomely in providing its desk officers a "feel" for the problems of the tactical elements who are the direct users of its products.

It is yet too early to make a full assessment of the value of this organization in terms of results versus cost. Indications at present are, however, that the CIS would be well worth estabishing in each Corps Tactical Zone during the coming year.

On my last day in Vietnam, I became aware that a new plan for attacking the Viet Cong infrastructure was to be implemented. It was to be called the Intelligence Coordination and Exploitation for Attack Against the Infrastructure (ICEX) Program. Ambassador Robert W. Komer was to head the program as a deputy to the MACV commander. To put it mildly, I was amazed and dismayed. I called on Mr. Komer and General Westmoreland that last day and pointed out that I had not known about the program but that I was confident that the combined military intelligence system was out front leading the way against the infrastructure. I suggested that co-ordination was in order.

POLICE FIELD FORCE FORMATION AT THE NATIONAL POLICE COMPOUND IN SAIGON *before a cordon and search operation with the 199th Light Infantry Brigade.*

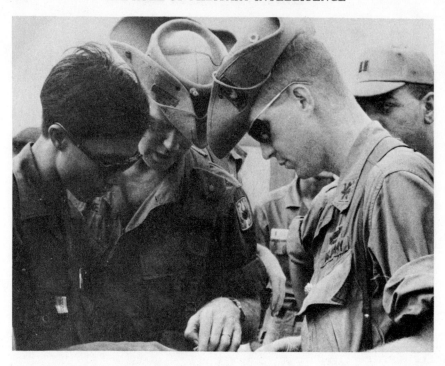

U.S. Operational Unit Commander in Charge of the Cordon and Search Briefs Vietnamese Police Officers, *above.* Screening Center Is Established With Photographs and Blacklist of Known Viet Cong. *Each suspect is brought to the center for preliminary interrogation, below.*

SEARCH TEAM IN OPERATION WITH SCOUT DOG AND U.S. SECURITY
ELEMENT. *Each team is composed of six Police Field Force members;
the security element consists of men from the 199th Light Infantry
Brigade, above.* SCOUT DOG WITH HANDLER *searching exterior of
dwelling and surrounding area for hidden persons and supplies, below.*

SEARCH TEAM AT HOUSE WITH U.S. SECURITY ELEMENTS ON LOOKOUT. *One member of the household is allowed to remain in the house during the search to insure that nothing is removed illegally, above.* POLICE FIELD FORCE SCOUT DOG HANDLER AND SEARCHER. *Each searcher is equipped with a steel rod used for probing, below.*

SEARCH ELEMENT WITH U.S. SECURITY GUARD LEAVING A DWELLING
AFTER SEARCH, *above*. POLICE FIELD FORCE ENTERING HOUSE TO CONDUCT
SEARCH. *These men were trained to search for hidden documents,
weapons, and other items which were stored in caches by the Viet Cong.
Each member of the household was also searched, below.*

SCREENING CENTER WAS ESTABLISHED AT A CENTRAL LOCATION WITHIN THE HAMLET, *above.* SCREENING CENTER IN OPERATION. *Suspects are questioned and photograph book is shown to co-operative individuals for assistance in identifying known Viet Cong in the hamlet, below.*

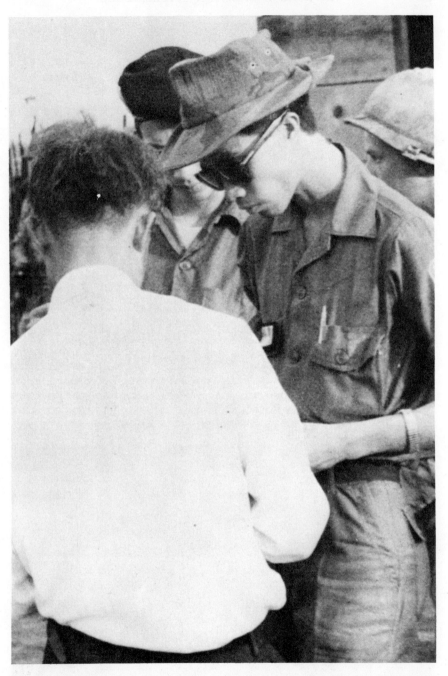

VIETNAMESE POLICE OFFICER WITH U.S. OFFICER *from the 2d Battalion, 3d Infantry, 199th Light Infantry Brigade, checking identification of a detainee.*

Police Field Force Reviewing Photograph Album in an Attempt To Identify Viet Cong in Hamlet. *The album contains photos captured during U.S. Operation Cedar Falls, conducted in February 1967, above.* Vietnamese Police Officer Checking Identification of a Suspect, *below.*

ADDITIONAL CHECKS OF IDENTIFICATION PAPERS BY VIETNAMESE POLICE OFFICIALS AT SCREENING CENTER, *above*. POLICE FIELD FORCE CHECKING HAMLET INHABITANTS AGAINST PHOTOGRAPHS OF VIET CONG SUSPECTS, *below*.

U.S. Representatives From Combined Intelligence Staff Conferring With U.S. Officer in Charge of the Cordon and Search Operation, *above*. Detainee Being Questioned by Police Field Force Personnel at Screening Area. *Suspect's name is checked against the blacklist, below.*

Vietnamese Officer in Charge Instructing New Officer on Procedures of the Screening Center. *Both are members of the Combined Intelligence Staff, above.* U.S. Civic Action Officer From the 199th Light Infantry Brigade Giving Treats to the Children. *In the same house, medical facilities have been set up to treat the sick, below.*

VIET CONG SUSPECT *being questioned by Vietnamese police officers of the Combined Intelligence Staff, above.* TWO SUSPECTS ARE DETAINED *from the large number screened during the operation, below.*

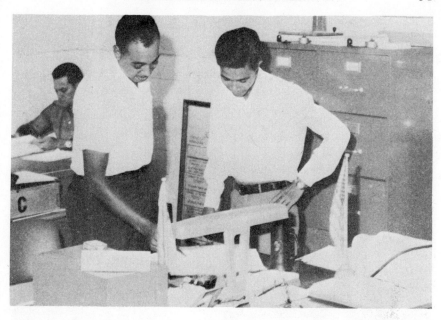

NHA BE DESK TEAM *discussing automatic data processing system input sheet before submitting completed work to the Combined Intelligence Staff, above.* VIETNAMESE CLERK IS TAUGHT PROCEDURES FOR COMPLETING AUTOMATIC DATA PROCESSING SYSTEM FORMS, *below.*

Vietnamese Chief of the Combined Intelligence Staff Conferring
With Deputy From the Office of the Special Assistant, U.S.
Embassy.

COMBINED INTELLIGENCE STAFF COMMUNICATIONS SECTION, *which maintained radio contact with all Saigon police precincts and districts of the area of operations, above.* DI AN DESK TEAM *checking blacklist against a list of apprehended Viet Cong, below.*

CHAPTER III

Combat Intelligence

Our combat units made contact with the enemy and evacuated prisoners, documents, and material. The combined centers furnished ever increasingly timely, accurate, and adequate intelligence. By concentrating on the eight order of battle factors, enemy capabilities and vulnerabilities were so accurately identified that the incidence of successfully determining his plans was surprisingly high. However, this war presented some rather unusual demands. One concerned political order of battle intelligence—more specifically, intelligence on the Viet Cong infrastructure. Because North Vietnamese forces were involved in South Vietnam, Military Assistance Command was required to monitor and report on Communist infiltration through Laos and Cambodia while providing order of battle data reflecting enemy units as regular, main force, local force, or guerrilla. The intelligence officer was asked not only to locate and identify the enemy but also to prove how he got where he was and where he came from.

During the early days (mid-1965) the few U.S. collection and exploitation activities were under the staff cognizance of the Intelligence Operations Division (IOD) headed by Colonel Glenn E. Muggelberg, whose vast experience in intelligence collection was invaluable. Faced with a growing demand for information, Colonel Muggelberg soon had almost everyone in his division functioning as an operator. Staff officers commonly went to the field to pick up an important captured document, to sit in on the interrogation of a key prisoner, or to examine an item of new equipment taken from the enemy. However, it was not long before individual efforts no longer satisfied the demand. At first, simple procedures were possible. We used a general collection plan for identifying requirements and resources and for assigning responsibilities. Separate directives were published in support of special collection programs.

Collection requirements normally were derived from tasks received from the production element. Close co-operation and co-ordination between the collector and the producer were essential. The producer knew what intelligence gaps existed. He had the data base and knew what information we already had. Within Military Assistance Command J–2 the Intelligence Operations Division, exploitation centers, and production agencies were located in different facilities. Co-ordination was achieved by placing representatives of the collection element with the producers at the Combined Intelligence Center, Vietnam.

Immense problems resulted from the huge increase in the number of specific intelligence collection requirements from our combat forces, Military Assistance Command headquarters, and Washington. Administrative tasks alone rapidly reached enormous proportions and prompted a need for an economic, yet efficient, management system without adding to the authorized manning level. Our solution was to incorporate collection management into the computer facilities of J–2. Utilizing four files, the system contained an inventory of valid collection requirements; approved essential elements of information and other intelligence requirements, orders, requests, and collection tasking; evaluated input from specified collectors; and served as a registry of all intelligence report numbers issued within Military Assistance Command. Known as the Collection Management System, it provided systematic coverage of the intelligence cycle: a data base reflecting the requirements, the reports that resulted, and an evaluation of the information contained therein.

My deputy for combat intelligence supervised the functions concerning J–2 air, reconnaissance, targets, intelligence operations, exploitation activities, and the Military Attache Liaison Office.

Aerial Reconnaissance and Surveillance

In the field of intelligence an important development has been the sophistication of aerial reconnaissance and surveillance. As a result of the remarkable advances in optics and electronic sensors, not to mention aircraft, we have barely begun to realize our potential. At one time we had, for example, the possibility of 112 different combinations of aircraft, sensor, and service that could be employed. Until the introduction of U.S. ground combat units in Vietnam in mid-1965, aerial reconnaissance and surveillance activities were concerned primarily with locating suitable targets for air strikes. The relatively small demand for close air support, together with an adequate number of aircarft for the situation at that time, obviated the need for a sophisticated tactical air control system. With the escalation of the U.S. commitment, rigid control of air assets became necessary.

Because of our interest in aerial reconnaissance, there was a requirement for the Army and Air Force to negotiate and establish a mutually acceptable system for control of air resources available to Military Assistance Command. In October 1965, a policy agreement establishing the Joint Air-Ground Operations System was promulgated. Based on experiences from Korea, the system combined certain aspects of the U.S. Air Force Tactical Air Control System and the Army Air-Ground Operations System but distinctly specified that control would be exercised at the joint (Military Assistance Command) level. This arrangement proved its worth and functioned effectively. Brigadier General Rockly Triantafellu, U.S. Air Force, then director of intelligence of the 2d Air Division, and his staff showed enthusiasm, and we were able to work in close co-ordination to develop the required systems. His successor at 7th Air Force, Brigadier General Jammie M. Philpott, was an equally dynamic and outstanding intelligence officer. These two officers deserve major credit for successfully developing our joint aerial reconnaissance and surveillance programs (*Appendix I*).

As an outgrowth of the Joint Air-Ground Operations System, it was necessary to create a joint operations center, subsequently designated the Combat Operations Center in deference to the Navy orientation of the theater commander, and to set up the other control mechanisms at lower echelons. Benefits accruing to J–2 were control and co-ordinating authority for photography, visual reconnaissance, and electronic intelligence (*Chart 13, Appendix J*).

The aerial reconnaissance and surveillance program played a vital role in the Military Assistance Command collection effort. Three complementary systems—photographic, visual, and electronic sensors—were among the primary sources of intelligence for the support of ground tactical operations, B–52 strikes, and interdiction of land and sea infiltration routes. Although eminently successful, this collection effort had some significant shortcomings and limitations. First of all, aerial reconnaissance and surveillance are dependent on environment. Cloud cover and jungle canopy reduce system effectiveness—visual and photographic. While electronic sensors such as side-looking airborne radar and infrared are operable under these conditions, bad weather often prevents aircraft from reaching the target area. During the seasonal monsoons that occur in Southeast Asia, there are prolonged periods when aerial reconnaissance or surveillance techniques are limited against key targets. Secondly, limited resources initially hindered the program. Also, the Republic of Vietnam was not the only area in

CHART 13—JOINT AIR-GROUND OPERATIONS SYSTEM

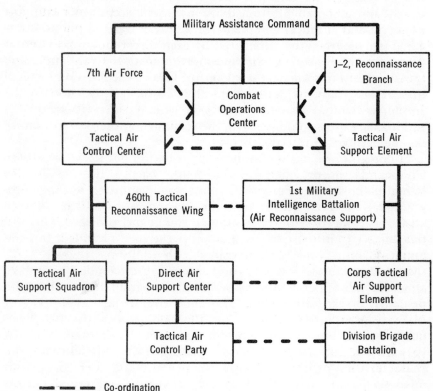

━ ━ ━ Co-ordination

which the United States had a requirement for aerial reconnaissance; the Commander in Chief, Pacific, and Strategic Air Command had other priorities that precluded the allocation of all their resources to Military Assistance Command. Consequently, Vietnam was never covered to the extent desired by the intelligence staff. Through the assiduous use of available joint resources, however, we managed to provide adequate support for the tactical units.

Tactical aerial reconnaissance was performed with optical (photographic), infrared, and side-looking airborne radar sensors mounted in Air Force RF101, RF4C, RB57, RC47, and U.S. Army Mohawk OV–1 aircraft. Missions stemmed from the monthly reconnaissance plan and daily requests. The J–2 Reconnaissance Branch monthly plan was based on requests and recommendations for repetitive coverage submitted by all major Army headquarters, the Military Assistance Command staff, and component commands. On an average, the plan included some 750 targets that were processed and assigned aircraft daily by the Tactical Air Support Element and Tactical Air Control Center. Daily requests—some 1,200 per month—were submitted by each direct air support center directly to the Tactical Air Support Element for validation and transmittal to the Tactical Air Control Center for Air Force execution. These daily requests were validated at each echelon in the Joint Air-Ground system to ascertain whether aircraft organic to subordinate units could perform the mission and thereby economize on the Air Force resources.

Photographic reconnaissance support for Military Assistance Command was provided by the 460th Tactical Reconnaissance Wing of the 7th Air Force. This unit was committed to other programs for the Commander in Chief, Pacific, and could not devote all its energies to Military Assistance Command projects. This did not detract from the quality of support the unit provided, but the quantity could have been increased with additional resources. Although many sorties were flown over South Vietnam daily, we were almost a subscriber to the photography program rather than the principal or executive agent. The same aircraft flew in support of Military Assistance Command and the Commander in Chief, Pacific; thus, the film casette from one four-hour sortie might contain very little of interest to Military Assistance Command. In fact, the characteristics of the high-performance aircraft used on photo missions permitted tremendous area coverage and raised doubts about the economic feasibility of point targets nominated by ground units. Stategic Air Command flew high-altitude photo missions in Southeast Asia and accepted Military Assistance Command mission requests; however, the climate and jungle canopy reduced their value.

The technological advances that have been made in optics (lenses and cameras), film, sensors, illumination, and methodology provided the greatest capability ever known. The biggest problem, mastering our technology and making the system work, was eventually overcome. Through the efforts of the Army, Navy, Air Force, and Marine Corps, we developed a magnificent photography program. In spite of potential charges of parochialism I extend a large share of the credit to the 1st Military Intelligence Battalion (Air Reconnaissance Support) (MIBARS), which greatly facilitated co-ordination of the photographic effort throughout the country.

Doctrinally, the 1st Military Intelligence Battalion (Air Reconnaissance Support) would be employed as an element of a field army to produce and disseminate intelligence information obtained or developed by Air Force reconnaissance aircraft, and its organization permitted deployment of a military intelligence detachment with each squadron of the tactical reconnaissance wing that customarily supported a field army. This concept had been tested extensively during field exercises in the United States and had been implemented successfully during the Dominican Republic crisis. However, the battalion, designed for conventional wars of the classic continental battlefield, had not been tested adequately in a counterinsurgency such as that in Southeast Asia, nor had it been in a prolonged combat theater.

The concept for the employment of the MIBARS placed the battalion headquarters at Tan Son Nhut with a detachment in each of the four corps tactical zones and thereby provided a direct support facility that would be familiar with the local situation. We became particularly satisfied with the arrangement, even though all the Air Force photography missions were flown out of Tan Son Nhut. By virtue of their personal contact with the reconnaissance wing and their close relationship with ground units, the battalion personnel contributed immeasurably to developing a truly joint effort in photo intelligence. Elements of the battalion and the 460th Tactical Reconnaissance Wing merged in order to provide the greatest capability. The rapport and mutual co-operation that evolved resulted in the 1st Military Intelligence Battalion (Air Reconnaissance Support) being one of the few Army units ever to receive a Presidential Unit Citation through Air Force channels. In addition, its many accomplishments were recognized when the 1st received two Meritorious Unit Citations.

Although numerous problems arose in the aerial reconnaissance and surveillance field, the personnel of the military intelligence battalion were extremely successful in overcoming them. Some of the first problems to be approached concerned education; there were almost no knowledgeable reconnaissance personnel in the Army. Too few commanders and staff officers knew how the aerial reconnaissance and surveillance system worked or appreciated what it had to offer. The battalion attacked these problems initially by publishing a comprehensive handbook that explained in detail its mission and how tactical units could request and receive support. In addition, Lieutenant Colonel Michael Tymchak, battalion commander, and his officers visited tactical units throughout South Vietnam to publicize the support their organization could provide to combat operations and how that support should be requested. Command-wide interest was thereby generated in the aerial reconnaissance and surveillance program. As the MIBARS gained experience and expertise, more ambitious measures were implemented. Lieutenant Colonel Eugene Kelley, Jr., who succeeded Colonel Tymchak, established schools for G–2 air officers and imagery interpreters. The course for air officers was designed to promote more efficient and effective utilization of aerial reconnaissance and surveillance resources by training men from the tactical units in the fundamentals and mechanics of the system. The imagery interpretation course was available to all imagery interpretation units in Southeast Asia, regardless of service, and was intended to provide the environmental orientation and familiarization that is so essential to accurate photo and imagery interpretation.

Another accomplishment of the 1st Military Intelligence Battalion (Air Reconnaissance Support) that was vital to the aerial reconnaissance and surveillance program was development and publication of comprehensive photo interpretation keys for Southeast Asia. These keys, actually a photo dictionary, were invaluable to the interpreters, and the over-all effectiveness and efficiency of the entire program increased when the keys became available.

One of the most significant missions undertaken by the 1st was Project WAYSIDE, a complex operation to produce annotated photomaps of selected areas in South Vietnam. The topographic map coverage we had in the early days was not accurate enough. While terrain features may have been correctly depicted, survey data and grids were only approximate. The MIBARS initiated Project WAYSIDE in an effort to provide photomaps of U.S. installations and areas in which military operations were planned. These maps proved to be reliable enough to permit accurate artillery support to be fired from map data, something that had been not always possible with the topographic maps previously in use. These photomaps became extremely popular and were in great demand.

These successes do not mean that the system was without fault. We never obtained a high enough priority to get all the equipment and support that the MIBARS needed and deserved. During my tenure as J–2, for example, we did not receive all the communications equipment authorized for the battalion. This lack contributed to the difficulties we experienced in attempting to provide more timely aerial reconnaissance support for the tactical units. A four- to seven-day time lag generally passed between request and receipt of photo, causing some criticism of our program, though there were instances of receipt within hours after request. An additional detracting factor was the lack of float aircraft for the battalion. When an aircraft was down for maintenance or other reasons, no substitute replaced it, and delivery of photos to supported units was delayed.

We also experienced considerable frustration in the area of logistical support for the aerial surveillance and reconnaissance program. The prime example concerns the ES–38 Mobile Photography Laboratory, a basic item of equipment that was essential to all photo interpretation units. There were no floats for the ES–38 in South Vietnam, and we were continually short of spare and replacement parts. Through the initiative of Colonel Kelley, the 1st Military Intelligence Battalion (Air Reconnaissance Support) became the theater-wide support facility for the ES–38's. His men literally became the technical experts on the equipment and played a key role in maintaining the Military Assistance Command imagery interpretation capability.

The visual surveillance program was conducted jointly by the U.S. Air Force, Navy, Marine Corps, Army aviation, and the Vietnamese Air Force. The nature of tactical operations demanded fully co-ordinated and repetitive coverage of border and coastal areas and other sites of high interest known to be utilized by the enemy in order to obtain real time reports of Viet Cong and North Vietnamese Army activity. The program varied from screening large areas for indications of enemy presence to concentrating coverage where ground operations were under way or patrolling over friendly troop movements. It included the capacity for directing artillery, naval gunfire, or air strikes on any targets, either fixed or fleeting, detected in the area of search. While helicopters supported the program at division level, the Army, Air Force, and Marine O–1 Birddogs (single-engine light observation aircraft) served as the backbone of airborne visual reconnaissance. Initially hampered by a shortage of aircraft, eventually we fully implemented the program with sufficient aircraft allocated to each corps to permit coverage of the entire country.

The corps were divided into visual surveillance areas governed in size by the area that one aircraft crew could cover in a systematic search during a two-hour mission. Frequency of coverage was influenced by the enemy situation, indications of activity reported by other sources, friendly operational plans, suspected enemy operations, weather, and aircraft availability. To make the program more effective, a pilot and observer covered the same area each day, developing in this way a familiarity with the terrain that facilitated detecting evidence of enemy activity (such as a new trail or road repairs). When necessary, or possible, a Vietnamese observer went along to permit communications with Vietnamese Army units in the vicinity.

As the program progressed, service responsibilities became more clearly defined. Air Force O–1's were assigned to tactical support squadrons, one of which was placed in support of each corps. These aircraft, however, were under the operational control of the Tactical Air Control Center through the corps' direct air support centers and were intended to perform in a forward air control role more than in one of visual surveillance; but they were available to support the reconnaissance effort when operational requirements permitted. This arrangement worked well as a result of the excellent rapport that existed among the corps staffs and their Air Force counterparts. The Army aircraft and crews were placed in direct support of the corps or division at which they were stationed. With their primary mission of supporting combat operations, the Army O–1's carried on visual surveillance, adjustment of artillery and naval gunfire, column cover, and radio relay. The Air Force Birddogs directed air strikes and, as a secondary mission, performed visual surveillance.

When the number of aircraft in Vietnam permitted, the sector was established as the basic echelon at which airborne visual surveillance was conducted. An aerial reconnaissance officer designated for each sector and division in each corps played a key role in the execution of the program. These officers supervised preparation of the reconnaissance plan, briefed and debriefed the surveillance team, and insured compliance with reporting requirements. To be of value the program had to provide timely information to the commander. An in-flight or spot report, used to disseminate information of immediate tactical value, could be sent directly to the support unit, division, sector, corps, or field force. The second report—an aerial observation report or debrief—was more deliberate. It completely detailed all sightings and observations during the mission and had to be forwarded to higher and adjacent headquarters daily. At each succeeding echelon, reports were consolidated and forwarded, ultimately reaching Military Assistance Command. Also, a weekly statistical summary submitted by each corps reflected aircraft availability, number of reconnaissance sorties, targets struck as a result of visual sightings, and surveillance areas not covered.

The employment of airborne radar and infrared sensors comprised a third aspect of aerial reconnaissance and surveillance. While the radar produced some very impressive results, readout of the infrared imagery presented a significant problem that was never adequately resolved. Before going to Vietnam, I had seen a demonstration of the microdensitometer in infrared readout, and the results convinced me it would be useful in Military Assistance Command. We ordered the equipment but discovered that it could not be used economically in Vietnam because of the complex, sophisticated installation process. Despite infrared problems, the OV–1 Mohawk (twin-engine reconnaissance aircraft) developed a reputation as an outstanding intelligence collector. The side-looking airborne radar was effective and, when used in conjunction with searchlight-equipped, armed helicopters, produced some remarkable results; for example, the LIGHTENING BUG operation where the OV–1 flew night patrols over waterways used by the enemy and then relayed the location and nature of lucrative targets to the waiting helicopters. The Mohawks were an integral part of the successful Military Assistance Command campaign to interdict the maritime infiltration routes used by the enemy. They provided infrared, radar, and visual coverage of large portions of the Vietnamese coastal regions in support of Operations MARKET TIME and GAME WARDEN, the patrolling and search of watercraft on inland waterways and the contiguous South China Sea.

As an adjunct to visual reconnaissance, and related to aerial photography, we initiated the hand-held camera program in an attempt to partially alleviate the timeliness problem since a mission could be flown, the film processed, the imagery interpreted, and the results delivered to the requester in a matter of hours instead of days. The program was implemented by the 1st Military Intelligence Battalion (Air Reconnaissance Support) for Military Assistance Command and by tactical air support squadrons for the Air Force. The MIBARS trained Army observers in the techniques of photography and also provided the cameras. Film could be processed at either the tactical units or the battalion. Several camera systems were tested. The first, employing the Questar lens on a camera chassis with motorized film transport, was unsuitable because of the need for a stable mount and the distortion that resulted from lens jitter when used in aircraft. The second system tested consisted of a catadioptic lens with 26-inch equivalent focal length mounted on the same body. Although compact and easily handled, the small aperture, limited depth of field, and critical focusing made this camera unacceptable. Further testing of off-the-shelf cameras resulted in selection of a Japanese model with a 200-mm. lens. For special application, we acquired a 500-mm. and a 1,000-mm. lens for use with the camera. Admittedly not the ultimate solution, it was adequate for our purposes.

The magnitude of aerial reconnaissance operations required that a system be employed to insure that data concerning missions flown and results obtained were maintained and readily available for retrieval. It was also necessary to provide information on specific items regularly as an aid for proper management of the program. With these broad goals in mind systems were established utilizing automatic data processing for storage and retrieval of information.

One system was used for the reconnaissance program within Vietnam. Experience with in-country operations revealed a need for information concerning the reconnaissance cycle, frequency and type coverage obtained, location of coverage, and results. Since intelligence resulting from missions is a production function, this informational need was incorporated into the Combined Intelligence Center, Vietnam, automated intelligence file.

From time to time it was necessary to determine what coverage was performed over selected areas in a given time frame. This could be done by sorting the cards by co-ordinate position and then printing out data from selected cards. The file could then be sorted by co-ordinates and dates to determine the results of the coverage obtained. This system was implemented in December 1966, and complete data were maintained after 1 January 1967. The results of missions outside Vietnam were also fed into the Combined Intelligence Center data base.

Automatic data processing provided a basis for collation of required data, rapid retrieval, and more accurate and timely statistical data needed for management purposes. Plans of the J–2 Reconnaissance Branch were formulated to improve the system. First of all, integrated data processing was to be initiated. This meant that the request for aerial reconnaissance would be in the format and coded so that all data were placed on the card which would be used for subsequent data reduction. Secondly, the Combined Intelligence Center would perform the data processing using the 1410 computer when the second machine became operational. This would allow tape storage and faster retrieval. The 27th Data Processing Unit maintained the in-country program in June 1969. Third, programs outside Vietnam managed by Military Assistance Command would be reduced to an automatic data processing system such as that applied to reconnaissance within Vietnam. This would provide a common base for data reduction so that the same type of information for all programs would be maintained in the same manner.

The importance of ground reconnaissance cannot be overemphasized. Ground reconnaissance not only can provide timely and accurate information on all aspects of the enemy and the area of operations but also can report on where the enemy and his influences do not exist.

The most professional and effective reconnaissance was performed by the 1st Australian Task Force. They conducted reconnaissance to collect intelligence and to avoid being discovered by the enemy. Their teams could remain on patrol for two weeks at a time without being resupplied. They were masters at it. Long-range reconnaissance patrols were employed at almost every echelon of command in Vietnam. These teams were good sources of intelligence for tactical commanders. Most patrols could direct artillery or air strikes on targets they discovered, but occasionally they called in such strikes at times when their continuous reporting on the enemy would have been more valuable.

Most patrol actions were planned, co-ordinated, and executed at the sector or division level. Some long-range reconnaissance patrols responded to Military Assistance Command and field force tasking. The marines could call upon their force reconnaissance unit in I Corps and the 5th Special Forces. The patrol capability was increased significantly by establishing the Military Assistance Command Recondo School at Nha Trang under the 5th Special Forces Group. I was highly impressed both by the Australians and by the successful night operations and reconnaissance conducted by the two divisions and the marine brigade from the Republic of Korea. The Vietnamese Civilian Irregular Defense Group border camps, which were isolated strongpoints advised by U.S. Special Forces teams, were located astride Communist infiltration routes. In addition to providing information about enemy movements and activities, these outposts conducted valuable reconnaissance and were a constant thorn in the side of North Vietnamese units operating in South Vietnam.

The employment of returnees (*Hoi Chanhs*) as scouts for U.S. units in the Kit Carson program was very successful. They assisted our patrols in locating and identifying enemy units and caches.

The Airborne Personnel Detector ("People Sniffer") signaled human presence by electronically detecting body odors. Unfortunately, inability to distinguish friend from foe limited its value in the ground mode, and it was more effectively employed when mounted in a helicopter and flown over areas known to be frequented by the enemy. Because aircraft thus equipped had to fly relatively low, vulnerability to ground fire was high and escort gunships were required.

Light intensifiers (Starlight Scopes) proved to be of great value in spotting enemy movement during darkness. Without the vulnerability of detection inherent in infrared light sources, the Starlight Scope intensified available light to permit observation.

While we have not yet realized the ultimate potential of unattended ground sensors, their use had considerable promise. Based on sonic, seismic, or pressure disturbances, sensors can detect people or vehicles and can transmit this information immediately to a monitor or store the data for subsequent readout by an airborne monitor. Again, these systems cannot discriminate.

There is no substitute for properly conducted ground reconnaissance. It takes men of great courage and physical stamina. It requires lengthy and intensive training. It requires miniaturized lightweight, dependable communications and aids to the human senses of sound and sight. Most U.S. ground reconnaissance was conducted to locate and conduct air or artillery strikes on enemy targets. Adequate emphasis was not given to avoiding detection, to maintaining contact, and to keeping the commander informed.

Operations

In the realm of area intelligence and the utilization of sensitive sources, initial plans called for an elaborate collection organization which could conduct shallow and deep operations. The original expectations proved overly ambitious and the program was reduced considerably. In addition, some jurisdictional questions arose from interservice disputes, hindering the establishment of an effective control mechanism. These were referred to the Commander in Chief, Pacific, and were resolved in favor of Military Assistance Command, creating a precedent for future controversies of this nature. However, relations with the Central Intelligence Agency were not covered by this decision, and while co-operation generally was excellent, J–2, Military Assistance Command, was not privy to all Central Intelligence Agency operations.

The collection effort concept initially called for a single command to conduct both unilateral and bilateral operations. Targets included enemy units and activities within the Military Assistance Command area of interest as well as special targets selected in response to local commanders' immediate needs for order of battle information. A large percentage of the effort established area coverage to satisfy better the requirements of tactical units. Generally speaking, these operations were moderately successful in answering specific requirements. Unfortunately most staff officers in intelligence slots lacked any specialized intelligence training, experience, or familiarity with the fundamentals of taskings for collection. The assignment to each sector headquarters and corps-level G–2 section of an intelligence liaison officer with the needed collection expertise partially alleviated the problem.

J–2, Military Assistance Command, was faced with an education problem within the military intelligence community in Vietnam. This problem also existed throughout the Army in general. Too few responsible people were familiar with area intelligence and how to use it. Security requirements may be cited by some as the reason for failing to include this as an Army mission at most service schools; but the Army cannot afford to classify itself out of this capability, and commanders must be made aware of its benefits.

Very ambitious programs targeted against the Viet Cong infrastructure and the Viet Cong irregular forces were initiated under the auspices of Military Assistance Command J–2. The focal point for these operations was at sector and subsector where the American S–2 adviser and his counterpart worked in co-ordination with local U.S. and Vietnamese intelligence activities. The primary objectives of these programs were to develop substantive data on the enemy political order of battle in support of the Military Assistance Command pacification and revolutionary development programs. Encouraging progress provided a foundation for the later, more expansive, Combined Intelligence Staff.

Some of the most active collection efforts utilized a technique described as specialized patrolling. Conducted by U.S. Army intelligence units and the U.S. Army Special Forces, these programs produced valuable information about enemy infiltration, troop movements, unit locations, and logistical facilities which helped develop accurate intelligence about the Communist military elements who hid in the base areas located in remote parts of the Republic of Vietnam. In some instances, impressive results were achieved which undoubtedly caused a diversion of enemy combat units to security missions. To increase the psychological pressures on the enemy soldiers and their infrastructure, we initiated programs to encourage defections among the Communist forces. Of course the government's *Chieu Hoi* program produced a large number of ralliers, who were, however, for the most part of little status within the Communist heirarchy. We devoted considerable emphasis to devising feasible means of obtaining defections among the top-level Viet Cong cadres and North Vietnamese military forces and sought to induce entire units to rally to the government of Vietnam. At best, we expected such programs to achieve only moderate success, and we would have been satisfied with merely reducing the morale and efficiency of a unit. Offering amnesty, for example, could cause the leaders to become distrustful of subordinates who did not devoutly follow the party line. We also used a rewards program whereby suppliers of information leading to the capture of high-ranking Communist officials were paid generously. These efforts did provide a commendable number of new sources for further exploitation; and regardless of reasons, returnee rates increased after the rewards offers were made. Funds also were made available to all commanders to pay rewards for enemy weapons or for information leading to the discovery of enemy caches.

An important factor in the intelligence effort was the role of the military attaches in Vietnam. In May 1964, with the growth of Military Assistance Command, the offices of the U.S. military attache were closed. Since a number of attache functions continued to exist, J–2, Military Assistance Command, assumed responsibility for many of the residual requirements, and several liaison officers were appointed within the Intelligence Operations Division to discharge the attache mission as additional duties. Later these functions were incorporated into the Foreign Liaison Office within the J–2 staff. Nevertheless, the growing attache requirements soon necessitated the expansion of our effort, and I established the Military Attache Liaison Office under Colonel Robert F. Robens as a division-level staff agency. The office was organized along the lines of a typical Defense attache office so that it quickly could assume the official attache functions. The Military Attache Liaison Office repeatedly proved its worth in co-ordinating matters pertaining to attaches from other countries as they affected U.S. forces and provided a diplomatic lever to secure information of value to the command.

Another aspect of our intelligence collection concerned the role of the U.S. Special Forces in Vietnam. As the Military Assistance Command combat organization expanded, efforts were redoubled to improve our capacity for conducting offensive intelligence missions in enemy-controlled areas, and we sought to take advantage of the vast potential of the 5th Special Forces Group. This organization, with A detachments strategically deployed throughout the country, had excellent communications from all units back to the group headquarters, its own airlift capability, and an extremely efficient command and control system. While the Special Forces was providing valuable input to our intelligence effort and was participating in some of our collection programs, it obviously could do much more. I visited the newly assigned commander of the Special Forces, Colonel Francis J. Kelly, in June 1966 and proposed a plan for using the potential of his group to collect intelligence of value to the entire command. Colonel Kelly enthusiastically received these recommendations and offered his full support.

To expedite the program I made available one of my most able officers, Lieutenant Colonel Richard L. Ruble, to be the first career military intelligence officer assigned as S–2 of the 5th Special Forces Group. The results were gratifying. First, a number of regulations were written to explain the steps necessary to improve the intelligence program, and mobile training teams were dispatched by the group S–2 officer to visit each A and B detachment to assist in their implementation. Marked improvements were observed in collection operations targeted against the enemy military and political order of battle. Production was advanced by the establishment of an intelligence analysis center in each corps tactical zone.

As intelligence tasking continued to expand, it became evident that additional personnel, particularly those with specific intelligence skills, were essential. Two augmentation units were provided: the 403d Special Operations Detachment and an unnumbered military intelligence detachment composed of 110 men. The 403d was retained under group control while the 110-man augmentation detachment was organized into five teams containing counterintelligence, interrogation, analytical, and administrative specialists. One team was retained at group headquarters and one sent to each of the group's four companies. With the deployment of these teams, the 5th Special Forces Group intelligence organization provided excellent finished intelligence to its subordinate units as well as higher headquarters. The sophistication of the intelligence apparatus allowed for operations against the infrastructure, particularly through the low-level informer nets that were established by the A and B detachments. In addition, an elaborate collection capability soon emerged and highly productive programs were initiated. Detachment B57, which was a 52-man unit; a 13-man special mission group; the 403d Special Operations Detachment; plus some 125 intelligence personnel stationed with the C detachments came directly under the group S–2. The men of the Special Forces were ideal intelligence collectors; they knew the value of intelligence.

The objectives of one special collection program in effect were to develop timely intelligence on North Vietnamese Army infiltration through Cambodia, the Viet Cong and North Vietnamese Army bases in Cambodia, and Cambodian support to the Viet Cong and North Vietnamese Army. All prisoners were interrogated concerning their routes of march from North to South Vietnam. If they were ever in Cambodia we asked for witnessed, handwritten signed statements from each source. His picture was attached to his statement. We had a book full of such evidence, much of it valuable. J–2, Military Assistance Command, published a detailed report on the role of Cambodia in supporting the Viet Cong and North Vietnamese Army. This program was highly successful.

Another program was designed to collect information on the Viet Cong infrastructure and to update the Viet Cong political order of battle handbook. This was a combined collection effort primarily at the sector and subsector level. By June 1967 about 15,000 names were reported as possible members of the infrastructure.

Another similar plan was directed at the development of an accurate estimate of the Viet Cong irregular forces strength, thereby providing a measure of the Viet Cong ability to increase their regular forces strength and to offset their regular forces losses. Such information also provided a better understanding of the problem facing the Republic of Vietnam and the U.S. and Free World Military Assistance Forces in their pacification and revolutionary development efforts. Again, the focal point of this effort was at the sector. By the end of May 1967 this program gave us for the first time a good estimate of the Viet Cong irregular forces strength. It had taken about five months. Colonel Loi and I had decided to place the requirement for this plan through our separate channels of communication. He tasked the Vietnamese intelligence officer at each sector to submit to him a report on the organization and estimated strength of the Viet Cong irregular forces. I requested the American intelligence officer at sector to furnish me the same information. Then Colonel Loi and I had our staffs compare reports. We resubmitted our requests and asked for full co-ordination of all agencies. Their eventual reports gave us the best information available to date. This was the first planned effort to collect such information.

Another J–2, Military Assistance Command, program was established to intercept suspect enemy trawlers and steel-hull ships bringing supplies and men into South Vietnam. This was primarily a Navy program, but all agencies participated. The program was very successful.

During the last sixteen months of my tour the number of active specific intelligence collection requirements had increased 146 percent and we were processing about 350 at all times. Also, the number of intelligence reports (Department of Defense Form 1396) from 1964 to 1966 increased 5,000 percent. Over thirteen thousand reports were handled in 1966. During the first four months of 1967 there were almost 9,000. From this proliferation of reports an economical, yet efficient, method to manage this administrative requirements was needed. The system developed for this purpose was named the Military Assistance Command Collection Management System and was a subsystem of the Military Assistance Command Intelligence Data Handling System.

The Collection Management System data base had four files. The first file contained all the information applicable to specific intelligence collection requirements, such as who originated the requirement, who had to collect the information, what was the priority of the requirement, and when the requirement expired. These requirements were generated by the Defense Intelligence Agency and other intelligence consumers. Data were provided monthly for both staff and field use in the form of a collection requirements registry.

This registry provided the collection manager with an inventory of active specific intelligence collection requirements and arranged these requirements in formats which enabled rapid identification by management-oriented groupings such as subject matter and geographic area addressed (for instance, North Vietnamese anti-aircraft tactics in the Central Highlands). The registry proved its value by accommodating the increased burden of requirements administration both at the headquarters and in the field. The registry, updated monthly, served as the specific intelligence collection requirement inventory and working control document for both.

Also from this file, every month, a separate report was provided each requirement originator. This report listed those specific intelligence collection requirements for which the originator was responsible which were due to expire and which therefore needed to be reviewed. The purpose of the review was to insure on the one hand that collection assets were not dissipated on satisfied requirements and on the other hand that valid requirements were not cancelled.

The second file was also a requirements file. It contained the essential elements of information and other information requests which the MACV commander had approved. It also included the indicators, specific orders and requests, and collection tasking for each essential element of information and collection requirement.

From this file we published the Military Assistance Command intelligence collection plan for the 1967 combined campaign plan.

The computer program available for processing this file permitted rapid updating of the requirements and republication of the document without burdening the field units with administrative details such as "pen and ink" changes. Plans called for this file to be placed on tape for easier updating and retrieval. We also intended to develop a system which would provide field units with a version oriented specifically for their use. This later system would become feasible as the J–2 computer capability improved.

The third file, the evaluation file, contained the opinions of a requirement originator as to the value of the information provided by a specific collector, for example whether it was timely, whether it answered the question, or its general value in the light of intelligence holdings. This type of evaluation is basic to successful collection. It is a form of feedback from which both the collection manager and the collector can analyze, redirect, and redefine their collection objectives. In effect the requirement originator or analyst provides a scorecard which measures the success of the collection action. It was estimated that approximately 40 percent of Military Assistance Command be evaluated and this percentage was an adequate sample for a valid evaluation program. It was envisioned that this file would be used primarily in-house by the collection managers in evaluating the quality of the reporting system.

The fourth file provided a registry of all intelligence report numbers issued for reporting purposes within Military Assistance Command. A significant portion of this file contained an expanded computer record which provided management data on those reports which had been evaluated.

This file did not contain the intelligence information provided by the report. Other files within J–2 contained the substantive intelligence data which had been reported. The reports which emanated from the file were used in monitoring and evaluating reporting activities to detemine the extent of response of specific requirements (specific intelligence collection requirements or collection plans, for example) and to determine the over-all extent of collector response to specifically assigned collection tasks.

The Collection Management System, through these four files, provided the collection manager with a useful tool for controlling, evaluating, and redirecting, where necessary, the collection effort. The system served the requirement originator, the manager, and the collector by providing a total system wherein the collection cycle could be traversed. It provided a data base from which information could be provided the originator, the collection manager, and the collector on all requirements levied on Military Assistance Command collection assets, selected intelligence reports submitted by Military Assistance Command collection assets in response to requirements, and evaluations of selected reports submitted by Military Assistance Command collectors.

Exploitation Division

The combined agreement of October 1965 between Military Assistance Command and the Republic of Vietnam Armed Forces established a combined exploitation system and provided for the establishment of physical plants to house each activity at national level. A second agreement concluded in June 1966 established similar provisions for materiel exploitation.

In order to implement the system, four intelligence exploitation programs were placed into effect. These were the interrogation, document, materiel, and *Chieu Hoi* programs. These combined programs, based upon the aforementioned agreements, had several factors in common. They were controlled and co-ordinated by J–2, Military Assistance Command, and J–2, Joint General Staff; they involved combined employment of U.S. and Vietnamese resources; and they aimed to achieve timely intelligence.

At Military Assistance Command level, staff supervision over these programs became the responsibility of the Exploitation Branch, Intelligence Operations Division. In February 1967, during a J–2 organizational realignment, the Exploitation Branch was broken away from the Intelligence Operations Division and was redesignated the Exploitation Division. The Exploitation Division exercised direct staff supervision over the Combined Military Interrogation Center, the Combined Document Exploitation Center, and the Combined Materiel Exploitation Center. The fourth exploitation program was the *Chieu Hoi* program, the purposes of which were to induce defection, to collect intelligence, to weaken the Viet Cong cause, and to convert the returnees to useful citizens.

Only those Viet Cong or North Vietnamese soldiers who defected after supporting the military or political activities of the National Liberation Front were eligible for the *Chieu Hoi* program. After being exploited for intelligence and after a period of reindoctrination and training, returnees were resettled as normal citizens of the republic. J–2 interest in the *Chieu Hoi* program was primarily in its intelligence potential. In 1966 it was estimated that only 10 percent of all *Chieu Hoi* returnees were being exploited for intelligence or psychological purposes. In July 1966, a concerted effort was initiated to improve the intelligence exploitation of returnees through the assignment of additional J–2 personnel to the program, including full-time J–2 liaison officers at each of the four corps. Exploitation improved to the extent that few returnees were overlooked as potential sources of information on the Viet Cong. All North Vietnamese Army and Viet Cong military cadres and all political cadres were evacuated to the national *Chieu Hoi* center in Saigon, where they were interrogated in depth.

Some representative cases that have occurred since August of 1966 illustrate the formidable intelligence potential of the program. The U.S. marines in the I Corps area implemented a program for the tactical exploitation of selected *Chieu Hoi* returnees. Identified as Kit Carson Scouts, military returnees who had completed the prescribed reindoctrination at a *Chieu Hoi* center were recruited from the centers and hired full time as guides or scouts for tactical units. Over thirty of these scouts were employed by the marines, and plans called for a total of fifty by June 1967. These scouts contributed to the success of search-and-clear operations and identified and assisted in the capture of over forty-five of their former Viet Cong compatriots. Similar uses of returnees in support of tactical operations were carried out in the other corps areas.

Since August 1966, three very important Viet Cong and North Vietnamese Army personnel have voluntarily returned to South Vietnamese control under the *Chieu Hoi* program. The first of these was Lieutenant Colonel Le Xuan Chuyen, the former chief of staff for operations and training of the 5th Viet Cong Division. He was highly knowledgeable throughout a broad spectrum of military subjects. In May 1967 Colonel Chuyen was appointed director of the national *Chieu Hoi* center in Saigon.

In October 1966 the assistant director of the Central Office of South Vietnam medical school, Nguyen Huu Hung, returned to government control. He provided a considerable amount of detailed information pertaining to Central Office personalities, order of battle, and medical training.

In March 1967 the former chief of the training section of Military Region V, Hoynh Cu, returned to government control. He provided valuable information on North Vietnamese Army strategy in the Western Highlands Military Region and on Military Region V organization and activities, logistics, and order of battle.

Based upon information provided by a returnee in the IV Corps area, the South Vietnamese Army 21st Division reacted by launching an immediate operation which resulted in 309 Viet

Cong casualties, 13 captured, and large equipment losses. These are some typical examples of the intelligence exploitation of the *Chieu Hoi* program.

The highlight of intelligence exploitation in 1967 was the quality, quantity, and timeliness of information gained as the result of Operation CEDAR FALLS, which was directed against Military Region IV from 8–26 January. To improve tactical interrogation during the operation, ten field interrogation teams consisting of a total of fourteen Americans and eight Vietnamese from the Combined Military Interrogation Center were sent to support the tactical units of II Field Force. Interrogations yielded valuable information on unit identifications and locations.

The operation proved to be an intelligence windfall in terms of captured enemy documents. Of the 492,553 pages received during the period, 52,797, or approximately 11 percent, were either summarized or fully translated. These exploited documents provided information regarding the subordinate units and agencies of Military Region IV, including defense plans for War Zone C. Also included was an outline plan and general objectives for the Viet Cong 1966–1967 campaign. There were strong indications that the entire military file on Binh Duong Province unit headquarters was captured by friendly forces. Over 1,500 pages of signal intelligence and crypto material were processed. These pages of crypto material included signal directives, signed operation instructions, and crypto operator notebooks, most of which were originated by the Crypto Cell, Current Affairs Committee, Military Region IV. The timely initial exploitation of these documents yielded tactical and strategic intelligence.

Two document exploitation teams consisting of four Americans and two South Vietnamese from the Combined Document Exploitation Center were in direct support of combat units. Timeliness of evacuation and exploitation was excellent. Capturing units were provided on-the-spot tactical document exploitation support, and the results of every document exploited at the center were provided to tactical units and to the Military Assistance Command staff within twenty-four hours.

On 22 February 1967 Operation JUNCTION CITY was initiated by units of II Field Force, Vietnam, and III Corps. Intelligence exploitation included the capture of a large quantity of film which provided excellent identification photos of members of the Viet Cong hierarchy. The take consisted of various positives, negatives, undeveloped exposed film, unused film, and some duplicate film. All of this film was processed, screened, summarized, and combined into a total of sixty-five reels varying in length from five to thirty minutes. With the co-operation of the Joint U.S. Public Affairs Office, five of the films were combined to make a composite 35-minute film with a commentary soundtrack added in English. This composite film depicted the late General Nguyan Chi Thanh visiting a hospital in Tay Ninh Province, South Vietnam; General Thanh was a member of the North Vietnamese Politburo and the commanding general of the National Liberation Front of South Vietnam. (In the summer of 1967, he was mortally wounded by a B–52 strike in Tay Ninh Province.) In addition, the film showed Major General (then Brigadier General) Tran Do addressing a meeting of the Central Office of South Vietnam; General Do was the deputy political officer of the National Liberation Front and chief of the political section of the Central Office. Generals Thanh and Do were positively identified by a returnee who knew them personally.

The intelligence exploitation programs provided rapid response in interrogation by the Combined Military Interrogation Center ranging from tactical through strategic areas of intelligence interest; in document exploitation ranging from summarizations to complete translations, as well as automated rapid retrieval of documents by subject area by the Combined Document Exploitation Center; and in materiel exploitation ranging from on-the-spot technical evaluation to complete analysis at the Combined Materiel Exploitation Center.

Operation Cedar Falls

While Vietnam provided many examples of the role of intelligence in support of operations, CEDAR FALLS is a classic. I conceived this operation and recommended it to General Westmoreland. This was the first corps-level operation in Vietnam and employed a multidivision force in the notorious Iron Triangle, some twenty-five miles north-northwest of Saigon. Initiated on 8 January 1967, the operation aimed at the capture or destruction of Headquarters, Viet Cong Military Region IV, and its base camps and supply bases as well as the 272d Viet Cong Regiment. The Iron Triangle had become a sanctuary from which the Viet Cong operated with impunity against Gia Dinh Province and Saigon.

Because of the importance of the security of Saigon, the capital city, I had ordered the initiation of Operation RENDEZVOUS, a concerted effort to gather information about enemy personalities, units, headquarters, and activities within Military Region IV. RENDEZVOUS utilized all sources of intelligence collection from short-range radio direction-finding equipment, side-looking airborne radar, infrared, agent reports, photography, long-range reconnaissance patrols, and reports from the Combined Interrogation Center, Combined Document Exploitation Center, and Combined Intelligence Center. RENDEZVOUS became the example of co-operation and co-ordination on a large scale by the entire military intelligence community. The combined centers provided specialized studies on suspected and known members of the Viet Cong infrastructure, pattern analysis of likely troop and logistics concentrations, and photo studies. Since Military Region IV was immediately subordinate to the Central Office of South Vietnam, we expected to capture the Central Office and Hanoi's plans affecting Saigon. Any disruption of Military Region IV would delay Communist plans affecting the capital.

By late 1966, an analysis of information obtained from RENDEZVOUS established patterns which convinced me that a quick strike against Military Region IV would not only prove tactically successful but would probably seriously disrupt the region.

One morning in mid-December 1966, fortified with overwhelming intelligence, I recommended to General Westmoreland that Operation JUNCTION CITY be postponed and that II Field Force attack Military Region IV. He directed that I brief Lieutenant General Jonathan O. Seaman, commander of II Field Force, who was then preparing to launch Operation JUNCTION CITY in War Zone C.

We briefed General Seaman and his staff that afternoon on the intelligence that had been gathered. He studied the facts and was impressed by what he termed a "most convincing presentation." General Seaman agreed to postpone JUNCTION CITY and go for Military Region IV. He realized that contact with large units would be unlikely but agreed that the capture of equipment, directives, and personnel of such an important headquarters subordinate to the Central Office was important to the security of Saigon and was a potential intelligence coup. This, together with the disruptive effect on enemy operations against Saigon, was a great opportunity. I reported the above to General Westmoreland in his office that evening. He picked up the phone and called General Seaman. He ordered CEDAR FALLS and arranged to meet with General Seaman and his staff the next day. Intelligence was "out front."

Enemy order of battle at this time included, in addition to Military Region IV headquarters, the 272d Regiment, the 1st and 7th Main Force Battalions, the Phu Loi Battalion, and four local forces companies, all operating within the area. The 9th Viet Cong

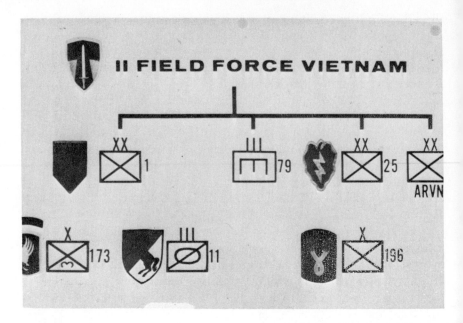

Task Organization for II Field Force, Vietnam, for Operation
Cedar Falls

Division minus the 272d Regiment was capable of piecemeal rein-
forcement within forty-eight hours from areas west of the Iron
Triangle. The enemy, however, was not expected to reinforce but
rather to defend supply bases and headquarters areas with available
security elements. His resistance was predicted to be primarily
delaying actions. Owing to the lack of friendly operations within
the area, extensive fortifications and tunnel systems also were
expected. Estimates of the enemy's strength and probable courses
of action proved accurate in that the 272d Regiment avoided
major contact and left the defense of Military Region IV to local
forces.

Immediately preceding CEDAR FALLS, tactical units deployed
under the guise of small-scale operations to sites within striking
distance of the Iron Triangle. Both the 1st Infantry Division and
the 25th Infantry Division started deployment on 5 January, with
elements of the 173d Airborne Brigade, under operational control
of the 1st Division, initiating Operation NIAGARA FALLS in the
Cau Dinh jungle between Highway 13 and the Thi Thinh River.
The operation, when terminated on 7 January 1967, left these
elements positioned for CEDAR FALLS. They constituted the hammer
of the operation. The 25th Division deployed the 196th Light

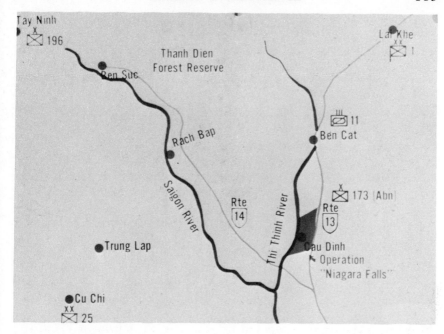

TASK ORGANIZATIONS FOR CEDAR FALLS WERE DEPLOYED WITHIN STRIKING DISTANCE OF THE IRON TRIANGLE, *above.* WHILE THE 11TH ARMORED CAVALRY DROVE WEST, THE 1ST DIVISION AND 173D BRIGADE WERE AIR-LIFTED INTO LANDING ZONES *around the edge of the Thanh Dien Forest Reserve at the northern flank of the Iron Triangle, below.*

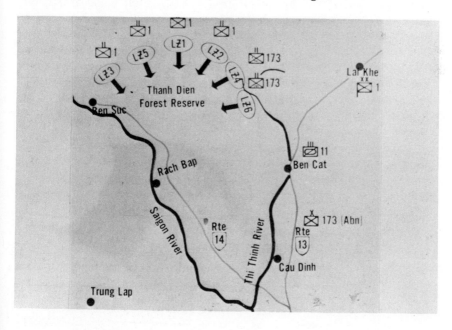

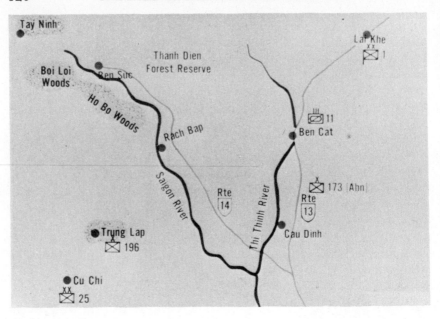

WITH THE MOVEMENT OF THE 196TH LIGHT INFANTRY BRIGADE FROM TAY NINH TO TRUNG LAP *and with the positioning of the 196th and the 25th Division near the Saigon River and the Ho Bo Woods, the anvil or blocking force for Cedar Falls was ready, above.* THE HAMMER OR STRIKING FORCE OF OPERATION CEDAR FALLS, *the 1st Division and elements of the 11th Armored Cavalry Regiment and 173d Brigade, struck on 9 January with the armor element driving west, below.*

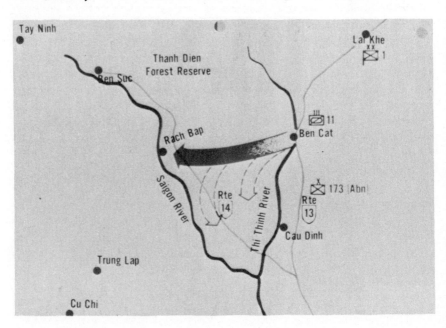

Infantry Brigade from Tay Ninh. The command post and trains of the 196th moved on 5 January to Trung Lap, southwest of the Iron Triangle. In the next two days the brigade shifted forces out of Tay Ninh and deployed four battalions into the Ho Bo woods close to the west bank of the Saigon River, and by 7 January they too were positioned as components of the anvil, or blocking forces, for CEDAR FALLS. Elements of the South Vietnamese 5th Infantry Division blocked on the southeast edge of the triangle. After heavy B–52 strikes against targets in the area which had been recommended by J–2 elements, the hammer or striking force of the operation, the 1st Infantry Division and elements of 11th Armored Cavalry Regiment and 173d Airborne Brigade, struck on 9 January 1967 with the armor element driving west out of Ben Cat to the Saigon River at Rach Bap. At the same time elements of the 1st Division and the 173d Airborne Brigade were airlifted into landing zones around the edges of the Thanh Dien Forest Reserve at the northern flank of the Iron Triangle for their mission, the destruction of the headquarters and related installations of the Viet Cong Military Region IV.

When the decision had been reached to attack Military Region IV, we were able to provide II Field Force with a wealth of intelligence on the area. This was accomplished in a matter of hours by using our two automatic data processing systems. The combined centers also were alerted to provide augmentation personnel to the tactical units on order. In the actual operations, teams from all the combined centers were dispatched to both the 1st and 25th Infantry Divisions for use as their commanders saw fit. However, in addition to the research and analysis support rendered by Military Assistance Command J–2, the intelligence units under our operational control also were tasked with providing support both before and during the operation. The 525th Military Intelligence Group supported CEDAR FALLS through subelements, including the 135th Military Intelligence Group, 149th Military Intelligence Group, and 1st Military Intelligence Battalion (Air Reconnaissance Support).

Detachment A of the 1st provided aerial photographic coverage of access routes and potential targets within the area. After the operation began, the detachment provided local support to the G–2's and S–2's of the divisions and separate brigades, working closely with the imagery interpretation sections of the military intelligence detchments, including seventy-six missions in support of the 173d Airborne Brigade alone.

The 149th Military Intelligence Group, which had been gather-

PRISONER OF WAR COLLECTION POINT FOR THE 1ST INFANTRY DIVISION *during Operation Cedar Falls, above.* ALL CIVILIANS IN THE CEDAR FALLS AREA OF OPERATIONS WERE DETAINED. *Thousands of refugees were screened each day, below.*

ing intelligence from Operation RENDEZVOUS for the preceding six months, provided specific collection support to Operation CEDAR FALLS as well. Representatives located with the intelligence sections of the divisions and separate brigades had the mission of assuring timely dissemination of information reports and keeping their headquarters advised of new requirements. Agents within the target area enabled the group to furnish information on the location of a munitions storage area, routes of march, and river traffic within the triangle.

Intelligence support organic to the five tactical units participating in the operation came from their military intelligence detachments and special operations units working with the divisions and separate brigades. Communications security teams also were deployed to the forward command posts to assist the commander in maintaining security of friendly communications. Prisoner-of-war and detainee interrogation sections established refugee screening camps in the forward base camps. All civilians within the area of operations were detained, and literally thousands of refugees were screened each day. Before deployment, the interrogation teams received detailed briefings from both order of battle and imagery interpretation personnel who provided aerial photographs with overlays for the interrogators to use as a base for questioning. Prisoner detention facilities were set up and counterintelligence and interrogation personnel worked in consonance. Counterintelligence personnel checked the blacklist while the interrogations were going on and obtained positive leads on many individuals who either provided information on enemy units and installations or proved to be Viet Cong themselves. They also accompanied local medical teams into the surrounding area and questioned the local populace for information on enemy intentions and dispositions.

Imagery interpretation and order of battle personnel worked together to provide hard targets to the attacking units. Month-old photographs of the entire area of operations were received from the 1st Military Intelligence Battalion (Air Reconnaissance Support). Apparent targets on these photos were rechecked and rephotographed by Army and Air Force aerial reconnaissance elements. New photographs were compared with order of battle holdings, and updated intelligence then was passed to the various G–2's for exploitation by infantry troops.

As a result of CEDAR FALLS, the Viet Cong command committee of the military region—consisting of the region commander and the chiefs of the military, political, and rear-service staffs—dispersed and were not heard from for a long time. In fact, friendly forces later produced the personal effects of these individuals including their wallets, toilet gear, and notebooks bearing top secret classification. The capture of the classified files of both the military and political staffs of Military Region IV seriously disrupted their efforts, as did the uprooting of the logistical operations and the capture of food and medical supplies.

In retrospect, CEDAR FALLS was nothing less than a significant victory in terms of casualties inflicted upon the enemy and materiel and rice stores captured or destroyed. More important was the vast amount of intelligence raw material that it produced. The term raw material is advanced advisedly, since many of the intelligence sources and documents turned up during the operation were usable on the spot by document exploiters and interrogators attached to the task force. Much of the exploitation of military intelligence, however, took place outside of the immediate tactical area—for the most part in the combined centers in Saigon.

General Seaman characterized this operation as the "biggest intelligence breakthrough in the war." During the course of the action in the Iron Triangle, 213 enemy were detained and, in addition, 512 suspects and 518 ralliers were held for interrogation. All the intelligence these sources provided was relayed at once to commanders in the field and to Military Assistance Command. Twelve valuable sources were sent to the Combined Military Interrogation Center for further exploitation by U.S. and South Vietnamese intelligence. Among the CEDAR FALLS detainees interrogated at the combined center was the operations officer of Military Region IV, who, in addition to being captured carrying about two pounds of documents, proved to be a lucrative source of information himself. Another important detainee, a high-level Viet Cong political cadre member, was initially unco-operative. He made the mistake of bragging about his background as a graduate of Moscow University, however, and the J–2 computers in Saigon soon produced his complete personal history statement. Many of the region intelligence files we captured had detailed accounts of its activities from 1962 to 1966; contained Viet Cong unit strength figures, personnel rosters, and areas of operation of specific units; and yielded valuable data on future operations. In addition, two thousand personal history statements of Communist cadre members were seized, leading to the arrest of a number of enemy agents operating in Saigon and other areas. Perhaps the most significant find was a copy of the 12th resolution of the Central Committee of the Communist party of North Vietnam which first announced direct intervention in the Republic of Vietnam by North Vietnamese troops. In all, over 490,000 pages of captured documents were sent to the Combined Document Exploitation Center; more than 52,000 of these were found to be of significant intelligence value.

Some 3,700 tons of rice—enough to feed five regiments for a year—were either destroyed or confiscated. Engineer elements, in addition to their massive jungle-clearing operations, destroyed over 1,000 bunkers, 424 separate tunnel complexes, and 509 structures. Seven hundred twenty enemy were killed and 555 individual weapons along with 23 crew-served weapons were captured between 8 and 26 January.

The Viet Cong themselves later admitted in highly classified reports that the operation constituted a disaster for them. The over-all intelligence value of the operation was unparalleled in the records of U.S. military efforts in Vietnam up to that time. Aside from all this, CEDAR FALLS was important as an outstanding example of the manner and means of intelligence support from the inception to the conclusion of a combat operation. The success of such operations in a war in which sound intelligence meant so much reflected the close co-operation between tactical units and the intelligence elements supporting them. All parties demonstrated a mutual understanding of requirements and the capabilities and limitations involved in the collection, processing, and use of intelligence.

CHAPTER IV

Intelligence Production

Collection efforts result in information. Until that information has been processed and converted into usable intelligence, it is of little value to a commander. When I arrived in Vietnam the weekly briefing being presented each Saturday morning to General Westmoreland was basically a current situation report which did not provide the intelligence he needed in order to employ effectively the combat power rapidly being developed in the Republic of Vietnam. The briefing was revised. We prepared an estimate emphasizing enemy capabilities and vulnerabilities. Our briefing normally culminated with J–2 recommendations for tactical operations to exploit enemy weaknesses or to spoil enemy plans. At the conclusion of the first revised briefing General Westmoreland gave his firm approval of this approach. He changed the purpose of the briefing to that of a strategy conference and limited attendance to his component commanders and key staff officers. Such a briefing took only fifteen to twenty minutes to present; but it took an extensive data base, a combined intelligence system, and the full time of a team of highly qualified estimators to produce. Colonel Loi and his staff also produced a weekly estimate, and our staffs compared our estimates. If any major differences surfaced I always included Colonel Loi's conclusions and reasons for the consideration of General Westmoreland. Such differences seldom occurred. Those weekly intelligence estimate updates were timely, accurate, adequate, and usable.

This example demonstrates the *raison d'etre* of intelligence—providing the commander with knowledge he needs. Converting raw information into meaningful intelligence is a complex procedure for trained analysts. Most Military Assistance Command intelligence analysts were young lieutenant graduates of the U.S. Army Intelligence School at Fort Holabird, Maryland. They were intelligent, educated, and energetic. They needed guidance but they learned fast. A few experienced officers at the Combined Intelligence Center gave them the guidance needed. They performed the vast amount of collation, evaluation, and production of enemy capabilities and vulnerabilities. They produced such studies in response to requirements originated by my estimators. They had to prove to the estimator the validity of every statement they wrote. Whenever I approved an estimate there was a vast amount of intelligence available to support every statement.

The Intelligence Division of J–2, Military Assistance Command, was responsible for intelligence production. The Combined Intelligence Center was under the supervision of this division. Four important branches within the Intelligence Division merit special attention.

The Current Intelligence and Indications Branch provided the MACV commander and his staff with significant current intelligence from all sources through daily briefings. In addition, the branch published the J–2 Intelligence Summary and the Weekly Watch Report. By virtue of access to intelligence from all sources, the Current Intelligence and Indications Branch was charged with producing studies and reports that could not be produced at the Combined Intelligence Center because certain sensitive information could not be released to other nationalities.

While most order of battle production was accomplished at the Combined Intelligence Center, the Order of Battle Branch of the Intelligence Division functioned as the primary point of contact within Military Assistance Command headquarters on all matters regarding ground forces order of battle. In this capacity the Order of Battle Branch had primary staff responsibility for developing command policy and preparing guidance concerning order of battle. With emphasis on composition, strength, identification, and disposition, the branch co-ordinated order of battle reporting and holdings with the Military Assistance Command staff, the Combined Intelligence Center, and the Vietnamese intelligence staff. By refining the product from the Combined Intelligence Center and incorporating other data available within Military Assistance Command headquarters, the Order of Battle Branch synthesized information from many sources and provided good, timely intelligence about the enemy.

Our order of battle reporting was reviewed by all members of the national intelligence community. Military Assistance Command statistics and holdings concerning the enemy forces often were questioned. Several factors contributed to this problem. Separate reporting channels existed between component commands and government agencies and their headquarters back in the United States. Everyone was forwarding order of battle information to his superiors in Washington without approval from the MACV commander.

A strong position concerning order of battle intelligence was necessary. We developed definitive criteria that governed Military Assistance Command order of battle reporting. These criteria had to be met before our holdings were altered. For example, we would not accept statistics concerning enemy troops killed by air strikes unless confirmed by ground reconnaissance, a prisoner, or a captured document.

On several occasions we were called upon to defend my order of battle criteria. First, a representative from the Office of the Secretary of Defense came to Saigon to examine and analyze our policies, criteria, procedures, and holdings. During his entrance interview he informed me that he had authority to order changes in my criteria and holdings. I told him that he would have full access to my entire organization and my full support, but that as long as I was Military Assistance Command J–2, those decisions would remain mine. Upon completion of his investigation, he strongly supported our methodology. No changes were recommended or made. Next, a team commissioned by the Joint Chiefs of Staff came to Vietnam to determine the validity of our statistics on enemy attacks contained in the J–2, Military Assistance Command, periodic intelligence report that did not coincide with statistics assembled in Washington. The team reviewed our order of battle files and traced the origin of the questioned statistics. Their findings supported our report. We reported finished intelligence; in Washington they had been using daily and weekly operational reports. Finally, in an effort to resolve once and for all the order of battle controversy, the Chairman of the Joint Chiefs of Staff directed that a conference be held in Hawaii to standardize the methods for developing and presenting statistics on order of battle and infiltration trends. Just before this conference I had published a Military Assistance Command order of battle manual on developing enemy strength. This manual contained all criteria, terminology, and definitions we had been using in developing order of battle holdings. This was the first of a series of order of battle manuals to be published. The conference convened on 6 February 1967 with representatives from the Central Intelligence Agency, Defense Intelligence Agency, National Security Agency, Office of the Secretary of Defense, Pacific Command, Military Assistance Command, and the component commands. Our order of battle manual was reviewed and readily accepted by all the conferees, thus vindicating our criteria and means of developing order of battle intelligence that had been in use since November of 1965. The Commander in Chief, Pacific, reproduced the manual and gave it wide distribution.

The most important part of the Intelligence Division was the Estimates Branch. This small, highly specialized group was created in late 1965. I worked very closely with my estimators and helped prepare all estimates. The questions they were asked to answer equated to: What is the enemy capacity to affect adversely the accomplishment of our mission? What are his vulnerabilities, and what is his will to persevere? Emphasis was placed on the quantity and quality of his available manpower.

The Estimates Branch became the focal point within the J–2 staff for all information regarding the enemy, and it enabled me to provide General Westmoreland with a continually updated estimate reflecting enemy losses, gains, trends in force buildup, combat effectiveness, capabilities, vulnerabilities, strengths, logistics, leadership, training, and morale.

Another branch of the Intelligence Division that played a key role in the Military Assistance Command intelligence effort was the Strategic Resources Branch. Focusing on domestic events and activities in the Republic of Vietnam, the Strategic Resources Branch kept the Military Assistance Command staff apprised of the political situation and related developments within South Vietnam. In the early days when governmental instability threatened the country, it was imperative that the MACV commanders and staff be kept abreast of fast-breaking developments during political crises. Such a situation evolved in March 1966 when the "Buddhist Struggle Movement" spread throughout the country and caused a virtual standstill in South Vietnamese military operations. The Strategic Resources Branch monitored the situation and dispatched daily situation reports as well as presented briefings as required. Also, the Strategic Resources Branch provided the point of contact for J–2 with the Military Assistance Command Office of Information, the Political Section of the U.S. Embassy, and the Joint U.S. Public Affairs Office.

Development and Publication of the Military Assistance Command Order of Battle Summary

The first issue of the Military Assistance Command J–2 Order of Battle Summary was published on 21 January 1966 and encompassed the period 15 December 1965–15 January 1966. It contained thirteen pages organized into a two-part format. Part I was a list of enemy units identified as main forces or local forces and as Viet Cong or North Vietnamese. Units were categorized according to the established Military Assistance Command and Republic of Vietnam Armed Forces acceptance criteria of confirmed, probable, and possible. Part II provided a recapitulation of enemy forces and total enemy personnel strength located in each corps tactical zone. In this first summary the total enemy strength was 79,500 in a force structure consisting of 29 regiments and 129 battalions. Of the 129 battalions, 77 were regimental and 52 were subordinate to provinces and military regions. In the ensuing months, the size of the order of battle summary increased proportionately with the increase in enemy strength and our knowledge of the enemy. Accepted enemy units in the first order of battle summary were listed on 8 pages. The list in 1967 required 40 pages to depict 9 divisions, 36 regiments, and 196 battalions.

After the publication of the first order of battle summary, additional sections were added. The section "Enemy Organizational Structure" showed the Viet Cong and North Vietnamese chain of command as it existed in South Vietnam. The maps showed the enemy forces located in each corps tactical zone as well as the boundaries of Viet Cong military and political organization. The section "Identification of Newly Reported Units in the RVN" provided a listing of all newly reported units and served as a watch list in focusing the attention of collectors on suspected units. Data on infiltration and retroactive strength were added to show the actual growth of the enemy force in South Vietnam. These data provided a true measure of the enemy's escalation of his war effort against South Vietnam. The section "Validity of Holdings for Enemy Battalions in RVN" provided a ready reference on the validity of each unit's acceptance in order of battle and "red flagged" those units which had disappeared from sight. Continuing effort was made to reconfirm the existence of units. Units which could not be reconfirmed were dropped if the total information on the unit and its area of operations left doubt of its existence. The section "NVA/VC Unit AKAs and Cover Designations" was one of the most useful and important sections of the summary. (AKA is an abbreviation for also known as.) The enemy's practice of redesignating units and using cover designations to deceive the allied forces was not successful. This listing provided users with reference material to relate an enemy unit's cover and alternate designations to accepted designations.

Besides the addition of these sections, formats were changed and revised continually for improvement. As a result of recommendations from Military Assistance Command J–2, the enemy force structure was recategorized as maneuver, combat support, administrative service, irregular, and political.

The summary's timeliness was insured by electrical dissemination of changes in the enemy's order of battle as soon as these changes were detected. A weekly summary cable, also dispatched electrically, recapitulated all information on current strength status as affected by changes which took place during the week.

Distribution of the order of battle summary increased steadily from 72 copies among 38 addressees to 425 copies among 75 addressees. This growth was indicative of the increased interest in Military Assistance Command order of battle throughout the U.S. intelligence community.

Development and Publication of Infiltration Statistics

The data base for the development of Military Assistance Command statistics on the infiltration of North Vietnamese soldiers into South Vietnam was maintained by the Combined Intelligence Center, Vietnam.

Captured documents, interrogation reports, agent reports, and tactical unit intelligence summaries were screened for information pertaining to infiltration into South Vietnam. This information was evaluated and used to compile statistics in accordance with the criteria of accepted, confirmed, probable, possible, or reported infiltration. Those North Vietnamese Army personnel, groups, and units which had entered South Vietnam and were carried either in the confirmed or probable categories were considered accepted. A confirmed infiltration unit or group was one which was accepted as in South Vietnam on the basis of information provided by a minimum of two prisoners of war or returnees from the unit or group, by two captured documents from the unit, or by a combination of personnel and documents. A probable infiltration unit or group was one which was accepted as in South Vietnam on the basis of information provided by one prisoner of war or returnee from the unit or group or by a captured document supported by information from other sources which could be evaluated as probably true. A possible infiltration unit or group was one which might be in South Vietnam on the basis of information which could be evaluated as possibly true even though no prisoner of war, returnee, or document verified the reports. Other units or groups which were mentioned in agent reports, captured documents, interrogation reports, or sightings by friendly forces were classified under reported infiltration; however, such information was insufficient to warrant inclusion into one of the other categories.

Infiltration statistics were discussed in detail at the intelligence conference held at Commander in Chief, Pacific, headquarters on 6–12 February 1967. It was concluded that infiltration statistics as then developed were based upon valid criteria and that Military Assistance Command would be the single source of infiltration data. To preclude confusion it was agreed that infiltration data would be cut off on the last day of each month and transmitted throughout the intelligence community on the first day of the following month. It was recommended that all agencies use these infiltration data in all reports, briefings, and releases until the next monthly report was received.

The conference further recommended that the Military Assistance Command monthly infiltration average be computed on a base beginning with October 1965. This beginning was decided upon as the most valid since it coincided with a period of substantial increase in infiltration and provided a sufficient data base on which to establish the average figure. Two averages were computed each month, one for accepted infiltration which included confirmed and probable, and one for the accepted and possible categories.

Enemy infiltration was such that it was difficult to detect many groups until after they had been in South Vietnam for as long as six months or even longer. This problem was compounded in 1967 because the enemy was forced to infiltrate greater numbers of replacements for his main force units. It was much more difficult to discover an infiltration group consisting only of replacements, which quickly blended into the existing force structure and lost their identity, than it was to discover a newly infiltrated battalion or regiment. For these reasons infiltration statistics were subject to continuing re-evaluation with the receipt of updating information.

Publication of Enemy Tactics Studies

In order to provide our combat units in Vietnam with information about enemy tactics I asked my staff to prepare a series of studies to assist the field commanders in developing measures to fix and destroy the enemy.

Our intelligence analysts reviewed and analyzed the existing information on Viet Cong and North Vietnamese Army tactical doctrine and past performance as reflected in captured documents, prisoner interrogations, and after action reports. In addition, they interviewed unit commanders, advisers, and troops in the field who had recently engaged in combat to draw on their experience. Eight analysts traveled to the field and interviewed small unit leaders and unit intelligence officers. These interviews were particularly valuable in that they provided us with recent firsthand experiences to include in the studies. Other significant information was obtained from translations of captured lesson plans and notebooks of Viet Cong and North Vietnamese cadres. These notebooks included information on the conduct of an ambush, the use of antiaircraft machine guns, and the employment of supporting arms. In addition, knowledgeable captives and returnees at the military interrogation center were interrogated. The former Assistant Chief of Staff Plans CT 5 VC Division was particularly informative in this regard. Information derived from other knowledgeable returnees, captives, and documents after the studies had been published were used to update existing information.

The product of this research was a series of hard-copy studies published in January 1967 to meet the immediate requirements of field commanders. Included were studies on the following:

Ambush tactics

Attack on fixed installations

Antiairborne and antiairmobile operations

Antiheliborne and antiairmobile operations

Antiaircraft defense by ground troops

Viet Cong and North Vietnamese Army night operations

Employment of snipers

Command and control of field units

Employment of guerrillas with local forces and main forces units

Night operations

Defense against armor

Reconnaissance tactics

River mine warfare

Crossing water obstacles

Command and control

Supply and resupply in combat

Employment of supporting weapons in attack and defense

Employment of guerrillas with local forces and main forces units

Viet Cong and North Vietnamese Army fire discipline

Enemy antiaircraft techniques, tactics, and employment

Viet Cong withdrawal tactics

Viet Cong evacuation of battlefield casualties
Viet Cong retrieval of weapons from battlefields
Viet Cong tactical use of inland waterways in South Vietnam
Viet Cong structures and field fortifications

Emphasis in the publication of these studies was placed on timeliness and accuracy of the material presented rather than on details of format and composition. Between eight and twelve hundred copies of each study were printed and disseminated to field commanders, the intelligence community, and U.S. service schools. Approximately ten thousand copies of tactics studies have been distributed since the program began.

Aerial Rice Survey of IV Corps Tactical Zone

An unusual project begun in December 1966 and completed in March 1967 was entitled "Aerial Rice Survey of IV Corps Tactical Zone." It was initiated and co-ordinated by the Strategic Resources Branch of the Production Division and was prepared by the IV Corps imagery interpretation team of the Combined Intelligence Center.

This study was initiated to determine the number of hectares of rice under cultivation within each province of IV Corps during the main 1966–1967 harvest period. This information was then compared with the November 1966 pacification area within each province by the Revolutionary Development Support Directorate so that a determination could be made of the number of hectares in areas controlled or contested by the Viet Cong. A determination was also made of the total number of hectares of row crops and orchards under cultivation within each province.

Because of the use of aerial photography, the results obtained were considered to reflect the true situation and provide a firm base on which to estimate rice production for the Mekong Delta region.

High altitude photography at a scale of 1:22,500 and 1:37,000 provided the basic coverage used in this study. Supplementary missions were flown to fill gaps in the basic photo coverage. The photography was accurately plotted on 1:250,000-scale maps and the rice-cultivated areas delineated on overlays of the same scale. The Itek rear viewer projectors and light tables with magnifying stereoscopes were used to select and define the ground areas under cultivation. Next the AR–85 Viewer-Computer was used to measure the cultivated areas on the photography. The areas under rice cultivation were delineated on the 1:250,000 overlays and were then transferred, using a Map-O-Graph, to a 1:500,000-scale map to present graphically the rice cultivation in IV Corps.

This study did not define those hectares on which two crops were grown annually. However, somewhat less than 5 percent of the total yearly production in IV Corps fell into this category. When using the estimate provided by this study, the double-crop areas had to be taken into consideration to provide a true production estimate.

Caution had to be exercised when comparing the imagery interpretation statistics for the 1965–1966 harvest season with those for the 1966–1967 season because of the variance in coverage available. The coverage available to the Combined Intelligence Center for the 1966–1967 harvest was 98.7 percent; that available for the 1st Military Intelligence Battalion, which interpreted the 1965–1966 harvest, was 97.1 percent.

No attempt was made to determine production statistics for the provinces. These computations were dependent upon accurate yield estimates, various types of crop damage estimates, and a determination of the area which had been double cropped. Such estimates fell within the expertise of agricultural specialists and were not in the scope of this study.

During 1966–1967, 1,543,007 hectares were under rice cultivation. This was 40,923 hectares less than the Vietnamese Ministry of Agriculture had estimated for the 1965–1966 harvest period. Of these 1,543,007 hectares, 579,045 fell within Viet Cong controlled areas and 415, 069 hectares were in contested areas. This left 548,893 hectares in areas secure to the government of South Vietnam. A total of 18,305 hectares was found to be under row crop cultivation, and 2,276 hectares were orchard areas.

The most significant difference found between the 1965–1966 and 1966–1967 harvest periods was the shift in rice hectares under cultivation from the provinces along the major waterways to provinces which have relatively minor waterways and which were predominantly under Viet Cong control. This change was believed to be a result of increased Viet Cong effort to raise production in areas under their control. Provinces predominantly under Viet Cong control in which production increased were An Xuyen, an increase of 8,935 hectares; Ba Xuyen, an increase of 23,577 hectares; and Bac Lieu, an increase of 44,630 hectares. Major decreases took place in those provinces which border the major rivers, specifically the Hau Giang, Co Chien, Ham Luong, My Tho, Mekong, and Cai Long and their tributaries. Provinces with the greatest decreases were An Giang, Chuong Thien, Dinh Tuong, Co Cong,

Kien Hoa, and Phong Dinh. The greatest part of the decrease could be attributed to the flood damage sustained in the fall of 1966.

Subsequent studies, using the graphics included in this study, would tell whether or not there was a change in the number of hectares under cultivation and where these changes took place.

In a telegram dated 29 April 1967 from the Secretary of State to the American Embassy, Saigon, this survey was cited by Mr. Rusk as being a most useful effort that provided sound bench marks to compare to future acreage estimates.

The Combined Intelligence Center
Imagery Interpretation Photo Study Program

In December of 1966 the III Corps Tactical Zone imagery interpretation team was tasked with making a photo study of the Lo Go area in Tay Ninh Province. The purpose of the study was to furnish photo intelligence on areas in which elements of the Central Office of South Vietnam had reportedly been operating. To accomplish this it was decided that, first, a detailed analysis of the photography would be made and all items of military significance identified and annotated on the photographs. Then, in order to establish the pattern of defenses, trail configurations, and proximity of collateral data to the items of military significance gleaned from the photography, a mosaic of the photos would be compiled. In the mosaic form the information extracted from each individual photograph began to form a pattern, particularly in the lines of communication and perimeter defenses. That is to say, instead of a trail simply spanning a single photograph, it could be followed from one photo to another and the entire defense system in an area identified.

Because the study consisted of twenty mosaics, an indexing system had to be devised that would allow the user to locate a particular mosaic without going through all of them to find the one of interest. To do this the mosaics were plotted on a 1:50,000 map and numbered. To show what intelligence items would be found on the mosaic, an overlay was prepared at a scale of 1:50,000 which reflected all lines of communication and defenses taken from the photography. The complete photo study package consisted of defense and lines of communication overlays, a 1:50,000 index to the mosaics, and annotated mosaics.

After briefing the field units on the photo study, it became apparent that its full value would not be realized unless it could be reproduced in sufficient quantity and appropriate format size to be distributed to each unit operating in the area covered by the study. The original size of a complete study was 30 by 40 inches, a size too large for field use. Arrangements were made at the 13th Reconnaissance Technical Squadron to reproduce the studies at a 50 percent reduction of the original size and in sufficient quantity to satisfy all requesters.

The reduced format was 15 by 20 inches and the mosaics were at a scale of 1:10,000 while the map and overlays were at 1:100,000. There was no appreciable loss of information in the reduction, and the smaller size was ideally suited for field use. The popularity and success of the Photo Study Program in III Corps led to its adoption as a product for all of the corps tactical zones in the Combined Intelligence Center, and in 1967 sixty-four such studies had been produced by the Combined Intelligence Center.

This type of study had a variety of uses. Special Forces units used the studies for setting up the security of their camps and hamlets. Advisory units used them in briefing and debriefing their counterparts and troops. Counterintelligence agents used them in the briefing and interrogation of indigenous agents. They were of immeasurable value in the planning and conduct of U.S. and Free World forces ground operations. In many cases the individual mosaics were removed from the studies and distributed down to platoon level for photo intelligence coverage of a platoon tactical area of responsibility. In addition to field uses, the photo studies were used by the Targeting and Strike Objectives Teams of the Combined Intelligence Center in determining targets for B–52 strikes and tactical unit objectives. In many instances the studies were used as a base for comparative cover from which ground activity was easily noted.

Starting from the receipt of the photography it took approximately fourteen days to complete and reproduce a study. Because of the great demand for the photo studies, it was decided that all original mosaics and the negatives made in the reproduction process would be held in a Combined Intelligence Center repository. These mosaics and negatives were on file in the corps team. Both the mosaics and the negatives were indexed and filed for easy retrieval. If a requirement existed for any single mosaic it could be retrieved and reproduced in a matter of hours.

The combined military intelligence system provided extensive and responsive collection and production. The estimator had the support he needed, and his support improved every day. The entire system existed to provide timely, accurate, adequate, and usable military intelligence to support sound decisions concerning conduct of the war.

CHAPTER V

Counterintelligence

Developing the Counterintelligence Effort

In mid-1965, the Military Assistance Command counterintelligence resources were quite limited. Under the staff supervision of the Counterintelligence and Security Division of J–2, Military Assistance Command, the 704th Intelligence Corps Detachment provided counterintelligence support to the command and served in an advisory role with the South Vietnamese Military Security Service. Essentially, this was the extent of our counterintelligence capability. Colonel George McCutchen undertook the development of an adequate counterintelligence organization.

With the reorganization of the J–2 staff in August 1965, the Counterintelligence and Security Division was redesignated the Counterintelligence Division with three branches: Personnel Security, Counterintelligence, and Security of Military Information. Counterintelligence operations continued under the 704th Intelligence Corps Detachment. In December 1965 Company B of the 519th Military Intelligence Battalion arrived in Vietnam and absorbed the mission, personnel, and equipment of the 704th.

In September 1966 the 135th Military Intelligence Group arrived under the command of Colonel Paul Goodman. The 135th assimilated Company B of the 519th Military Intelligence Battalion and assumed responsibility for executing the Military Assistance Command counterintelligence mission.

Continuing the example set by his predecessors, Colonel Goodman worked closely with the Military Security Service, and excellent counterpart relations existed. The increased counterintelligence capability permitted the deployment of counterintelligence teams to each province of South Vietnam. Often collocated with local Military Security Service elements, these teams participated regularly in combined operations. Close co-operation was essential to the success of our counterintelligence effort. The lack of linguists and the inability of occidentals to blend inconspicuously with the Vietnamese made combined operations not only desirable but necessary. Since we required interpreters and translators as quickly as possible, we had to rely on Vietnamese who knew English.

In order to conduct effective counterintelligence operations without infringing upon the sovereignty of the government of Vietnam, official agreements between Military Assistance Command and the Republic of Vietnam Armed Forces outlining the parameters of our authority to engage in counterintelligence operations were negotiated.

Throughout 1966 the counterintelligence program gradually improved. The mission grew considerably in November of that year when the Combined Intelligence Staff became functional. Combined operations expanded. By mid-1967 a sophisticated counterintelligence apparatus extended to all parts of South Vietnam. Counterintelligence services were available to every Military Assistance Command element and we were continuing to improve the effectiveness and efficiency of our programs.

Counterintelligence Operations

Counterintelligence Instructions Number 1, published in March 1966, was the initial effort to implement a Military Assistance Command counterintelligence standing operating procedure. As operations expanded, problems arose concerning command and staff relationships within the counterintelligence apparatus, area responsibilities, release and exchange of counterintelligence information, funds, and source control procedures. The instructions were revised and reissued, and in November 1966 work was begun on preparing *Counterintelligence Instructions Number 2.* However, the problems presented by the different geographic areas of Vietnam hindered the development of procedures that would apply without exception throughout the country. Consequently, the concept was changed and the Counterintelligence Division started preparing a command guide that would become effective in mid-1967.

Within the Vietnamese armed forces, the counterintelligence mission was assigned to the Military Security Service which did not fall under the control or staff supervision of the J–2, Joint General Staff, Colonel Ho Van Loi. In a Ministry of Defense directive issued in August 1965, the Military Security Service was given full responsibility for counterintelligence, while organic intelligence elements of other agencies were restricted to "pure" intelligence activities. Counterintelligence information collected other than by the Military Security Service was to be funneled into its channels. All intelligence agencies that became aware of information pertaining to sabotage, subversion, or proselyting were obligated immediately to notify the Security Service so that appropriate investigative or punitive action could be initiated. This policy probably was intended to achieve more effective utilization of collection and expolitation resources, a goal which proved elusive well into 1967. Because of its over-all orientation on domestic affairs, however, the Military Security Service retained a great interest in political reporting. Yet despite its interest in activity against the regime, we received co-operation from the Military Security Service to the extent of stationing U.S. personnel in its offices. I enjoyed fine working relations with Brigadier General Nguyen Ngoc Loan, who headed the service as well as the National Police. I respected him as a dedicated and professional officer.

To facilitate co-ordination of counterintelligence activities among the U.S. component commands and to promote interservice co-operation, the Counterintelligence Division established an orientation course for counterintelligence personnel. Navy and Air Force representatives taught the organization and mission of their respective units, and the curriculum included classes on the operations of friendly law enforcement and counterintelligence agencies in Vietnam, hostile intelligence agencies, the infrastructure, operational principles of counterespionage, counterintelligence targets, conduct of special operations, source control, and the missing U.S. personnel and prisoner program in Southeast Asia.

Education, as an effective measure for harmonizing joint counterintelligence efforts, was equally applicable to combined programs. Thus, in August 1966, the Combined Intelligence School stressed counterintelligence operations directed against the infrastructure.

The effect of enemy propaganda on U.S., Vietnamese, and allied personnel was of particular concern. Considerable propaganda had been directed by the Communists against U.S. servicemen. In 1966, combined operations in the III Corps area had been deluged by Viet Cong leaflets which, while purporting to provoke disaffection and defection from within the U.S. ranks, subtlely reminded the Vietnamese that their American counterparts might be vulnerable, since these leaflets included a Vietnamese translation. To help counter this activity all enemy propaganda material was collected and analyzed in co-operation with the U.S. Embassy, which retained authority for developing counterthemes to be used for counterpropaganda psychological exploitation of enemy weaknesses.

Upon entry into the Republic of Vietnam, all arrivals received comprehensive security orientations, including descriptions of hostile intelligence methods and military security. Since U.S. armed forces in Vietnam were a prime target for enemy intelligence efforts, everyone was reminded, through the initial and subsequent orientations, of his responsibility for reporting any observed suspicious activity and was told how and to whom to report.

Security inspections, liaison visits, and counterintelligence physical security evaluations were conducted throughout the command in order to remind our personnel continually to practice security.

The Military Assistance Command installation security program was directed at preventing sabotage. We defined sabotage and forwarded the definition to Pacific Command. We developed a specific directive to cover countersabotage operations. Contingency countersabotage plans were prepared for strategically important areas such as Saigon. We assessed potential vulnerabilities and advanced countermeasures to eliminate them. For example, we prepared a detailed plan for the physical security of the fifteen power facilities in the Saigon electric loop system. This planning involved conducting vulnerability assessments for all Saigon power facilities during the period 20 March–4 April 1967. The assessment evaluated guard forces, alarm systems, perimeter lighting, physical barriers, and other essential elements ordinarily part of a regular physical security survey. The over-all physical security of the facilities was judged "fairly good," though vulnerabilities such as poor lighting and families living within compounds were apparent. Both the MACV commander and the Mission Council were briefed on the project. The study concluded that the Viet Cong did present a constant threat to the facilities, with an even more likely target being the power lines in Saigon's periphery. Since power loop security was deemed in essence a civil matter under the aegis of the Vietnamese authorities, it was suggested that the U.S. Agency for International Development, which had both police and public works advisers counseling the Vietnamese, be designated the logical agency to have primary responsibility for insuring adequate maintenance for the physical security of the power facilities.

As an outgrowth of these early efforts to protect the Saigon power system, the Combined Security Committee was established under the directorship of the Chief of the Saigon Municipal Police to safeguard U.S. and allied personnel and installations against Viet Cong terrorism. Measures such as the ones taken on behalf of installation security began to manifest a co-operative spirit evidenced not only on the governmental level but among the people as well. Thus, the Citizens Incentive Rewards Program was used successfully in support of security functions by enlisting the cooperation of the Vietnamese public to report Communist terrorists, sappers, and the like.

In April 1967 another directive established criteria for designating critical and key installations in Military Assistance Command. A critical installation by definition was one of "such vital importance that its loss or severe damage" would entail "unacceptable delay or reduction in U.S. ability to wage war" or "cause major revision in the overall tactical planning of the war." Loss of a key installation would, in general, hamper U.S. ability to continue the conflict. Appropriate commanders were assigned responsibility for these installations. Commanders without an organic counterintelligence capability were enjoined to request assistance from their next higher headquarters.

Security of Military Information

The disclosure program in Vietnam for releasing classified information to our allies was a significant development that had great bearing on U.S. policy for security of military information. Our policy was based on the concept that the combined intelligence program demanded a free exchange of classified information among all participants—that intelligence personnel sitting side by side, working on the same project, and fighting the same enemy should have equal access to all available data. A lesser policy could only hinder our efforts to seek out the enemy, foster mistrust, and inhibit the maintenance of mutual respect and confidence. As a first step, maintaining classified information that could not be released in any of the combined centers was forbidden. This step drew criticism from many of the Americans involved in the combined program because they insisted that such data were essential to their jobs. Consequently, a list was prepared of all documents vital to the combined intelligence mission bearing the NOFORN (no foreign dissemination) caveat. We sent the list to the Defense Intelligence Agency with the request that it be reviewed with a goal of deleting the caveats. This procedure was time consuming, but eventually almost every document on the list was approved for release. For other than NOFORN information, my efforts secured an exception to national policy that gave General Westmoreland broad authority to disclose intelligence information classified through top secret, both Department of Defense and non-

Department of Defense originated, that pertained to hostile activities in Southeast Asia. Release would be based on the need to know as determined by the U.S. element concerned. This represented a breakthrough in the combined intelligence program and greatly facilitated operations.

In implementing the disclosure authority, the Counterintelligence Division published memoranda to serve as guides for the J–2 staff in providing information to our allies. One officer within each division was designated the point of contact for releasing information to allies. Anyone within a division might bring to him the documents to be released. If uncertainties about releasing the materials arose, the point of contact had recourse in the Counterintelligence Division where the disclosure officer, appointed by the division chief, would resolve the problem. No mandatory requirements dictated that dissemination automatically be approved; in fact, a prerequisite was that some benefits would accrue to the United States as a result of the disclosure. Upon receiving a request for permission to release classified information, the disclosure officer determined if current criteria were met. If not authorized, he informed the requester of the rationale for denial. The Disclosure Office maintained files of all disclosures, and the point of contact in each division kept records of any disclosures he had allowed.

Security of military information was the focal point for a significant intelligence effort in the Republic of Vietnam. The employment of local laborers on all military bases complicated the security program. Further, the tremendous increase in U.S. units and the expansion of the U.S. role brought forth an avalanche of classified documents and material. The need for an accurate accounting system was obvious. After a command-wide inventory of classified documents was initiated, the Counterintelligence Division instituted a program to reduce the number of secret and top secret items held by U.S. units in Vietnam. Command emphasis was applied to encourage the reduction in classified inventories. A monthly report was required to show the number of classified documents on hand at the beginning and end of the reporting period, the number of new documents generated, the number destroyed, the number dispatched, and the number downgraded. Within the Military Assistance Command staff, security control officers were required to attend a special training course before assuming their security duties. This training, besides making them knowledgeable of Military Assistance Command security policies and procedures, stressed supervision of security measures and practices within the staff offices and continuous security education.

Execution of the document security program was the responsibility of a field grade officer obtained specifically for that task from the Military Assistance Command Adjutant General. With a counterintelligence team of seven agents, he conducted inspections, and security checks to ascertain and evaluate compliance with Military Assistance Command security regulations, provided technical assistance, and supervised the training of the security control officers.

If the classified documents required intensive protection, so too did the information which they contained. In October 1965, a counterintelligence directive focused attention on security of classified operational plans. All major Military Assistance Command activities involved in operational planning were made responsible both for compartmentalization of various elements of the planning staff (minimizing complete familiarity with any given plan) and for insuring that individual elements of the over-all plan were not disclosed to persons not having a verified need to know. Procedures were thus commanded for the activities to effect situations to afford each element only that information necessary to prepare its component part of a plan.

Interest in security permeated all levels of the tactical and advisory chains of command. The rather simple, unsophisticated character of the enemy disguised his complex, highly efficient intelligence system. The insurgents' use of informers and agents could have limited the allied effort. Further, it is doubtful that the average U.S. officer or enlisted man ever appreciated the extent of the Communist collection effort even though the Counterintelligence Division placed maximum emphasis on educating them to the security hazards confronting the command daily.

The extensive use of local Vietnamese in administrative, logistical, and custodial services made U.S. facilities vulnerable to penetration and presented a serious challenge to the counterintelligence program. We alleviated the problem somewhat by requiring that Vietnamese full-time employees receive a favorable personnel security investigation from the Military Security Service, but hiring hordes of unscreened day laborers for construction and similar tasks constituted a continuing danger. Command attention was focused on the threats to security, and detailed, extremely restrictive directives served to remind all personnel of their security responsibilities. Widespread use of counterintelligence services, particularly inspections and technical surveys, improved the security posture of the command. Announced and unannounced inspections revealed inattention to basic security in the early days, but improvements noted in subsequent inspections indicated that our security education programs and increased command interest were achieving some success.

Even though Military Assistance Command was a joint headquarters, Army Regulation 380–5, *Safeguarding Defense Information,* was used as the basis for the command information security program, and a directive was prepared to adapt the statutory requirements to the situation in Vietnam. We had to insure that the information was available to those who needed it; therefore, the protective measures had to be realistic, yet achievable. For example, storage requirements were modified to fit the capabilities of tactical units and advisory teams. Another aspect concerned security classifications and marking. Because of combined operations with the Vietnamese, it was to be expected that a common need existed for access to sensitive data. A compatible security system was essential in furtherance of the combined concept. We agreed to honor each other's regulations and to afford the required protection to each other's classified information. To avoid confusion and preclude the mistaken impression that all information was freely exchangeable, security classifications were marked only in the language of the originator or proponent of a document. In a similar vein, all the allied forces in Vietnam accepted each other's personnel security policies. The multinational complexion of the military establishment demanded unquestioning co-operation among the members.

The Counterintelligence Division also was charged with developing the original files on Americans who were reported as missing in action or captured. The value of such records is evident. Precise biographic and identification data facilitated the evaluation of reports of prisoner sightings and assisted in refuting or confirming North Vietnamese and Viet Cong announcements about Americans who were being detained. The escalation of the U.S. effort, particularly the increase in missing and captured men as a result of the air war, eventually made the task unmanageable and the Counterintelligence Division was relieved of this responsibility.

I believed that censorship such as General Dwight D. Eisenhower exercised in World War II should be instituted. I requested that experts be placed on temporary duty with me in Saigon for planning. Three outstanding Reserve officers, Colonel James J. McHale, U.S. Air Force Reserve; Lieutenant Colonel Benjamin Goldberg, U.S. Army Reserve; and Commander Charles Heinbockel, U.S. Naval Reserve, were made available to me. They prepared draft plans for armed forces, civil, and prisoner of war censorship. These plans were completed in March 1966. They were furnished to all sections of the Military Assistance Command staff and component commanders for detailed planning and through the Commander in Chief, Pacific, to the Defense Intelligence Agency for information. The decision was never made to impose censorship; however, we were ready.

Communications Security

The day I became J-2, I requested and received general staff responsibility for the formulation of policy governing communications security. The signal officer was to establish such security within J-2 policy. All other staffs were made responsible for reviewing their activities for security considerations. Security of communications, as a result, proved mainly an administrative matter for the J-2 staff: It provided guidance and tasking to the communications security support elements of the Service cryptologic agencies in devising plans for supporting Military Assistance Command and the component commands; it validated third-country requirements for communications security material; and it promoted a staff visit program to check adherence to communications security policies and procedures at all echelons. In the meantime, the signal officer's staff had many practical concerns such as insuring that communications systems installed and operated by U.S. forces met the published security standards; advising Vietnamese and other commanders on the design, installation, and operation of communications systems to achieve communications security objectives; and formulating plans for introduction of new security equipment or material in Vietnam.

Within the Vietnamese Joint General Staff, the J-7 had responsibility for communications security and the J-2 had only an intelligence liaison mission.

With the increased U.S. activity, security malpractices were bound to multiply. The Counterintelligence Division wasted little time in developing standing operating procedures designed to enhance security. The first directive was published in October 1965 and covered conventional telephone and voice communications. The telephone, a convenient transmission medium whose extensive and common usage was required by the urgency and number of daily actions, represented a potentially prolific and reliable source of intelligence for an enemy. In addition, telephone conversations within Vietnam to terminals outside the Saigon area were transmitted by radio besides being routed through switchboards operated by or accessible to local nationals. We directed staff officers to become "aware of the vulnerability of the telephone and, within their respective sections, insure through supervision that personnel remained security conscious when using the telephone." In December another directive–incorporating the "out front" philosophy–enhanced communications security, compelling that communications security requirements be considered during the planning phase of all types of operations, to include methods and procedures to protect communications from enemy exploitation. Component commanders were enjoined to develop and institute communications security programs and provide the Counterintelligence Division copies of implementing instructions.

Cryptographic security was singled out for special attention, since it was "one of the most sensitive and closely held categories of classified information." Unless specifically authorized, U.S. advisers employing operations codes were implored not to store such material lower than battalion level and then only under augmented provisions. Unauthorized access to cryptographic information constituted a serious hazard bordering on compromise, which had to be reported as a physical security violation. Indeed, both allies and civilian employees were considered in a different light when seen through the eyes of communications security specialists: providing communications security aid to foreign governments was allowed only after approval and guidance had been extended by national communications security authorities. Prerequisite consultation through channels to the Counterintelligence Division proved necessary before such assistance became available to allied forces.

A different appreciation for communication security raised some problems. For example, the same sensitive operational information passed by secure means in U.S. communications might be transmitted concurrently over the telephone by an allied element. Even within our own forces there were instances of partial disregard for security when commanders sometimes failed to observe all the communications standards. Still, considerable progress was made in the field of communications security and the Counterintelligence Division achieved commendable success in improving the over-all communications security posture of the command.

CHAPTER VI

Intelligence Support

Management

As the Military Assistance Command intelligence organization grew, we sought managerial tools that would facilitate supervision of our many programs. On 30 August 1965 the formation of a management division was directed.

First, we sought to overcome the lack of continuity within the intelligence staff that resulted from the policy of one-year tours. Two courses of action were followed. First, we produced directives and memoranda to cover recurring functions and enjoined every officer to keep a functions manual that could be passed to his successor, insuring a ready reference designed to answer questions about his job. For those functions that crossed divisional lines, a directive was published. Next, we promoted continuity by encouraging key people to extend, and many at all levels did.

The Comprehensive Intelligence Program, developed to provide a means for keeping abreast of the status of J–2 staff actions, was first initiated at a time when more than 150 major projects were under way, and management problems were many. The program centered around production of a review and analysis chart maintained by each action officer for each of his projects. The chart briefly described the project and its objectives, status, trend, analysis, and actions. From this record a graph reflecting monthly activities plus a brief synopsis sheet was produced. Later redesignated the Review and Analysis Program, the Comprehensive Intelligence Program provided summarized data by which the progress of all J–2 functions could be assessed. This important management tool enabled us to foresee possible problem areas and prescribe corrective action before intelligence capabilities suffered.

Repetitive measures for improving the efficiency of the Military Assistance Command intelligence organization and the J–2 staff were necessary. In May 1966 a management survey was initiated in J–2 to identify those areas in organization, functions, and staffing that required modifications to accomplish assigned functions. Through this medium the soundness of the J–2 organizational structure was insured, the delegation of responsibilities and assignment of functions were facilitated, and the incidence of duplication of effort among the divisions and branches was reduced.

One of the most perplexing problems faced by the military intelligence organization in Vietnam concerned the timeliness of reports. We sought to instill in intelligence officers at all levels an appreciation of the importance of getting information to field commanders in sufficient time for them to act upon it. I required that every information report include a timeliness block. Each officer who initiated a report had to record the time he made the information available to the commander who could act on it. My special assistant, Captain Strachan, monitored these actions and notified me when they were not timely—a procedure which precipitated an admonishment to the responsible officer. Rapid transmission of intelligence information proved always a matter of prime interest, and the J–2 staff grew very proficient in the expeditious dispatch of "hot" reports.

Of all the techniques, procedures, or managerial tools employed by Military Assistance Command J–2 in the continuous campaign to improve efficiency, speed up processing, and expedite dissemination of intelligence, automation undoubtedly was the most valuable. The unlimited potential of computers presented a real challenge to the imaginative and innovative spirit of the intelligence staff, and maximum effort was devoted to adapting intelligence functions to these machines.

As G–2 of U.S. Army, Pacific, I had conducted an extensive educational program on automation for my staff in Hawaii. I had also become familiar with the FMA storage and retrieval system. I wanted to establish automation as soon as possible. My requests for equipment, trained personnel, space, and funds fell on unsympathetic ears. I received no help. I knew what I wanted, so I requested Pacific Command to survey my needs. They supported my requests, but it would take many months to fill them.

However, I discovered within the J–2 staff Lieutenant Lilly, who was enterprising in addition to being IBM trained. After a general discussion about the desired capability he set out to accomplish his mission. The first obstacle he encountered was the refusal of the Adjutant General's office to accept intelligence input because of classifications. However, the visit to the Adjutant General's office was fruitful in another way; Lieutenant Lilly salvaged a card punch machine that had been damaged in shipment. He repaired the machine himself, then trained an operator, and the

J–2 staff at least could punch its own cards. Later he discovered a computer van being used in conjunction with imagery interpretation. He arranged its transfer to Tan Son Nhut where, placed in a shed at the Combined Intelligence Center, it became the J–2's first computer facility. Little by little, additional equipment fell into our hands, much of it scrounged, enough so that in February 1966 the automatic data processing system began operating. Some months later, plans were included for the acquisition and installation of a computer within the J–2 area of the new Military Assistance Command headquarters under construction near Tan Son Nhut. After ascertaining the special construction necessary to install the equipment programmed for use by the intelligence staff, Lieutenant Colonel Edward M. Gudely was detailed to co-ordinate with the engineers and insure that the computer requirements were incorporated into the plans for the building. The J–2 area within the new headquarters was built to accommodate the modern equipment on order that would contribute so importantly to the accomplishment of the intelligence mission in the years to come.

The fiscal accounting and supervision of Intelligence Contingency Funds was another Management Division concern and one which I considered extremely important. Before 1 January 1966, this support for Military Assistance Command was provided by the U.S. Navy. These funds were identified by the Navy as Collection and Classification of Information funds, and their use was limited to the support of the Military Assistance Command intelligence advisory activities of the Republic of Vietnam. U.S. Army and Air Force intelligence activities were provided funding support by their parent organizations at the theater level. Control and administration of Collection and Classification of Information funds left much to be desired from both an administrative and an operational point of view. I had no control over the Intelligence Contingency Funds support for Army and Air Force intelligence activities since their reporting channels were to their parent organizations located outside the Republic of Vietnam. Responsive fund support slumped behind in the rapidly changing operational situation, encumbered as it was by extremely long lines of communication to the support base. Centralized control over intelligence operations was inadequate because each operating intelligence unit funded its own operations. This, in many cases, contributed to the lack of effective co-ordination of intelligence operations.

I knew that the most effective means to control intelligence operations was to control the purse strings. To this end I requested the assignment of Lieutenant Colonel (then Major) Autmer

Ackley, Jr., to my staff to set up an Intelligence Contingency Funds Class B Agent account. Colonel Ackley was appointed the Class B Agent, and the account was activated on 1 January 1966. At the same time a standing operating procedure was published which provided for the administration, supervision, utilization, and control of Intelligence Contingency Funds within the Republic of Vietnam. A similar standing operating procedure applicable to the Collection and Classification of Information funds was published at the same time, and supervision of these funds also came under the direct control of Colonel Ackley. The advantages of this centralized control were readily apparent: all intelligence operations required J–2 staff approval before funding support could be provided. In addition, funds were now immediately available to me for the fullest exploitiation of targets of opportunity such as high-level defectors and the Volunteer Informant Program.

Fund support of all intelligence activities in the Republic of Vietnam was now under my direct control with the exception of those activities sponsored by the Air Force, which maintained an independent fund support channel. A higher degree of professionalism as well as a more rapid response to intelligence requirements resulted from this centralized control of fund support.

In addition to the problem of decentralized fund control, the acquisition of intelligence equipment of all types, from small cameras to extremely expensive intelligence production equipment, presented major obstacles. In practically every case, intelligence units arriving in Vietnam came equipped with items of intelligence equipment completely unsuited to their missions there. It was necessary that the right equipment be obtained and issued to using units as rapidly as possible. I directed Colonel Ackley to establish an intelligence equipment control point which had as its mission the control over procurement and distribution of all intelligence equipment in the Republic of Vietnam. This activity was established on 1 February 1966, and through it we were able to shift equipment between units to use it to the fullest and to satisfy operational requirements.

The operational influence provided by the Intelligence Contingency Funds and the Collection and Classification of Information funds and by intelligence equipment resources being directly under my control allowed a more rapid and effective response to tactical requirements. Specialized equipment could be—and was in some cases—procured in a matter of hours and placed in the hands of the user. The primary lesson to be learned from these operations was that provisions for Intelligence Contingency Funds and special equipment support should be established in the joint command headquarters as early as possible. As long as operational control is retained at joint staff level, fund and equipment control must be located at that level also. I owe much to the dedication, perseverance, and expertise of Colonel Ackley in establishing and managing this vital program.

Finally, a daily staff conference to facilitate co-ordination of efforts within the military intelligence community for avoiding duplication and to keep me advised of the current intelligence situation was necessary. The conference served as a forum to air problems and elicit the expertise of the intelligence staff in resolving these problems. The Military Assistance Command science adviser, Bill McMillian, at my invitation became an enthusiastic daily participant in these conferences and attempted to have implemented many ideas for new equipment and techniques that arose there.

The J–2 concept for the organization of the Military Assistance Command Intelligence Data Handling Systems was based upon the requirement for two separate facilities because of security restrictions. These facilities would be mutually supporting. The first was for production processing of releasable data using automatic data processing equipment at the Combined Intelligence Center and the use of FMA Filesearch equipment for the automated storage and retrieval of documents at the Combined Document Exploitation Center. The second was for processing of sensitive data from all sources within J–2 using both automatic data processing equipment and the FMA Filesearch equipment.

The development of the J–2 Intelligence Data Handling Systems began in the fall of 1965 when an FMA Filesearch automated document storage and retrieval system was requested to provide a rapid means to retrieve data from interrogation reports and translated captured documents. This equipment was put into operation at the Combined Document Exploitation Center and by June 1965 had the largest microfilmed data base of any FMA system in the intelligence community. Over 9,000 feet of microfilmed documents were included and on file at the Combined Document Exploitation Center.

This system was highly successful, and the usage factor indicated that a second set of the same equipment was needed. A set was ordered in January 1967 with delivery expected in May. This equipment was put in operation at the Combined Document Exploitation Center as an interim location until it could be moved to the J–2 area of the new Military Assistance Command headquarters. The two sets of equipment would make J–2 able to handle releasable documents at the Combined Document Exploitation Center and nonreleasable or sensitive documents within J–2.

To be able better to disseminate and exploit this indexed microfilm, a 16-mm. reproduction camera was ordered. This would enable us to copy the FMA indexed microfilm and disseminate 16-mm. film cartridges to field units and other intelligence users. Thirty-five 16-mm. reader-printers were also ordered for distribution to these users.

In February 1966 automatic data processing operations started with borrowed electrical accounting machines installed in expandable vans parked next to the Combined Intelligence Center. The first equipment used was the basic punch card accounting machines. Twelve files were initially selected for machine operations that would provide the most immediate payoff.

In August 1966 the Combined Intelligence Center received an IBM 1401 card computer and additional peripheral equipment. In January 1967 a second small card computer, an IBM 1130, and a 1627 plotter were added to the equipment. Also in May 1967 the IBM 1401 computer was upgraded to a 16K memory with six magnetic tape drives. This more than doubled the center's production capacity. At the same time the IBM 1131 computer was upgraded to a magnetic tape system that could provide machine listings and plot simultaneously.

We chose to provide automated support to the nonsensitive data base at the Combined Intelligence Center first since it had the greatest application that could be disseminated to the most users.

In the area of automatic data processing support for J–2 and the sensitive data, the Commander in Chief, Pacific, and the Defense Intelligence Agency concurred in a second computer facility for J–2 in the new Military Assistance Command headquarters building to process nonreleasable and sensitive data. An IBM 1401 computer was the minimum equipment that would meet J–2's immediate needs. However, this would provide for only limited expansion. Therefore it was anticipated that the Defense Intelligence Agency would approve a larger computer, either an IBM 1410 or an IBM 360 model.

Within the J–2 Management Division there was an Intelligence Data Handling Systems branch with two sections, an FMA section for automated document storage and retrieval and an automatic data processing section. In the Combined Intelligence Center there was an automatic data processing branch. The Intelligence Data Handling Systems Branch of the Management Division provided guidance to Combined Intelligence Center automatic data processing and Combined Document Exploitation Center FMA. The future J–2 Intelligence Data Handling Systems organization contemplated a division with an automatic data processing branch of two sections, one for J–2 and one for the Combined Intelligence Center, and an FMA branch with two sections, one for J–2 and one for the Combined Document Exploitation Center.

The Management Division also was responsible for supervising the construction projects for various Military Assistance Command J–2 and Joint General Staff J–2 activities. The construction program for J – 2 encompassed approximately $6.7 million. Of this amount $3.7 million was programmed for the construction of eighteen combined interrogation centers. The balance of $3 million was programmed against the Combined Intelligence Center complex. The eighteen combined interrogation centers were located from as far north as Hue to Bac Lieu in the south. The program encompassed three different-size facilities. The largest, the Combined Military Interrogation Center, was funded at $450,000 and was located in the Saigon area. This facility, which had sixty-one permanent detention cells, including two temporary holding cells, became operational on 30 November 1966. Final cost for the structure came to $1 million.

In addition to the Combined Military Interrogation Center, three corps-size facilities were programmed for Bien Hoa, Pleiku, and Da Nang. The corps center was somewhat smaller than the combined center in that it had only a 26-man cell capacity. The cost of these facilities was programmed at $246,000 each. The corps center at Da Nang, near Marble Top Mountain, was to be completed by late August of 1967.

The remaining fourteen interrogation centers were division size and were referred to as combined division interrogation centers. The capacity of each center was to be an 18-man cell block. The facilities were costed at $182,000 each. The center at Ban Me Thuot was completed and officially accepted by the Joint General Staff on 26 April 1967. Construction started on the center at Hue on 1 April 1967. The remaining twelve centers were in various stages of construction—design or acquisition of real estate, for instance—in June 1967.

The Combined Intelligence Center complex construction started in late January of 1966, and the facility was occupied on 10 December of that year. A photo lab in the rear of the center was under construction. In addition we requested that the Combined Document Exploitation Center be expanded by approximately 4,500 square feet.

Future J–2 combined construction requirements envisioned the construction of a Military Security Service complex. The request along with the basic plans was submitted and approved.

Plans and Training

Two principal duties were assigned to the Plans and Training Division. The first was the J–2 input to the Combined Campaign Plan which set forth the priorities, goals, and objectives of Military Assistance Command, the Republic of Vietnam Armed Forces, and Free World Military Assistance Forces for the conduct of the war. Within J–2 we recognized the Combined Campaign Plan as an excellent vehicle for promoting the combined intelligence concept, and the Intelligence Annex was prepared in a combined effort by Colonel Loi's and my staffs. The professionalism and excellence reflected by the Intelligence Annex elicited high praise.

A second function of the Plans and Training Division concerned mapping, charting, and geodesy. The scope of Military Assistance Command interest in mapping and charting extended to Army topographic maps, Air Force aeronautical charts, Navy hydrographic charts, and survey control data (an Army responsibility) as well as numerous related products necessary to support combat forces such as terrain studies, flight information publications, gazetteers, and tide tables. In area, the primary concern was the South Vietnam land mass and its immediate tactical zone, although all of Southeast Asia was included in the program.

With the relatively suddent increase in tactical units, the demand for maps skyrocketed. An initial stock of some three million maps and charts was obtained from the map depot in Japan and was combined with the maps on hand in the Military Assistance Command Training Aids Section. At the same time, two Engineer topographic units, the 569th Engineer Company (Topography) (Corps) and the 547th Engineer Platoon (Map Depot), were brought to Vietnam to develop the Military Assistance Command charting, mapping, and geodesy capability. In the interim, direct air shipments from the United States together with continued support from Japan enabled map requirements to be met.

By October 1966, map stockage met the needs of the command. In April 1967, the new 1:250,000 Joint Operations graphic map series began arriving, with coverage of North and South Vietnam, Laos, and most of Cambodia by the end of May. This map was received in two versions, one for ground use and the other for air operations. In mid-1966, the very popular pictomap started to arrive in Vietnam. It was a photo-based, color-intensified map supplement produced at a scale of 1:25,000, intended for use by the small unit leader. Captured maps were particularly important since Viet Cong place names often varied from the South Vietnamese government designations. Because of their value during interrogations, Viet Cong maps were reproduced in monochrome print and distributed to selected users in the intelligence community.

Weather

Meteorological services were provided to Military Assistance Command by the Southeast Asia Joint Operations Weather Center via three media: oral briefings, including a weekly briefing for General Westmoreland; a daily written and pictorial weather forecast for South Vietnam and all of Southeast Asia; and specific daily weather forecasts for individual ground operations in the Republic of Vietnam. Weather support for major combat operations was provided by U.S. Air Force combat weather teams of the 5th Weather Squadron that prepared tactical forecasts. The excellence of the over-all meteorological program evoked praise from General Westmoreland to the effect that "no other U.S. military commander ever had the advantage of the outstanding weather support which I had at my disposal."

In the early days we had a serious problem in trying to get sufficient weather data to permit the preparation of accurate forecasts and to maintain data on current conditions throughout the country. The solution was surprisingly simple but extremely successful. We again called upon the Special Forces to provide a service vital to the command—weather reporting. The A detachments deployed within all corps were ideally suited for submitting weather data. It was a relatively simple task to train the Special Forces personnel in gathering the information, and their excellent communications facilities permitted rapid submission of reports.

CHAPTER VII

Summary

The intelligence challenge in Vietnam was more than finding the enemy. The challenge was providing timely, accurate, adequate, and usable intelligence in support of decision makers from the Military Assistance Command commander and his battlefield commanders to the Commander in Chief in Washington. An organization designed to meet that challenge was created. It established for the first time in history a combined military intelligence system. It took longer to establish that system than it should have because, once again, we were not prepared.

A few of the many lessons I learned, some for the umpteenth time, follow.

Unity of Command. One of the long-accepted principles of war—unity of command—was violated in Vietnam because of the nature of the insurgency. In this conflict, all U.S. intelligence organizations were not centralized under the MACV commander.

Combined Intelligence. Contingency plans should include draft agreements; standing operating procedures; organizational, functional, and manning concepts; and logistical support plans to establish a combined intelligence system, preferably including all military and civilian agencies.

Combat-Ready Intelligence Force Structure. The force structure of the services must include the combat-ready intelligence structure to support contingency plans. Such forces should be engaged in collection and production activities during peacetime as well as wartime. They should be capable of deployment on very short notice and should arrive in the area of operations with all equipment and facilities required. Time is precious.

Order of Battle. Order of battle is the foundation of combat intelligence. Order of battle training in the U.S. Army has been deplorable for many years. Military intelligence officers should have been trained on enemy units, weapons, and tactics, as well as on the Viet Cong infrastructure.

Human Intelligence. Among the best sources of combat intelligence are knowledgeable informants and captured documents. The drastic cutback in resources and training devoted to human intelligence since World War II has seriously reduced our capacity in this field. Officers slated for key command and staff positions should be educated on the advantages and limitations of this aspect of military intelligence.

Tactical Training. Our forces must know the tactics of the enemy on the battlefield where he will be fought. We did not have that knowledge when we were committed. Our combat units were not properly trained to maintain contact with the enemy once it was made. Consequently, we did not fix the enemy so that he could be destroyed on the ground.

Reconnaissance. Reconnaissance provides eyes and ears for the commander. The intelligence officer should have staff supervision over all reconnaissance, including ground reconnaissance.

Communications. Intelligence requires the timely movement of extremely large volumes of words and pictures. Dedicated communications in support of intelligence are a necessity. Automated systems designed to display elements of intelligence in a format are good if capable of reflecting the human analysis essential to valid intelligence. The human needs a data base. The data base requires communications.

Initiative. Intelligence officers should be imbued with the necessity to provide intelligence and appropriate recommendations upon which plans and actions are initiated rather than just to respond to requests for intelligence.

"Scouts Out." When I enlisted in the Army I was trained as a scout of a rifle squad. When the command "Scouts Out" was given I ran forward with my rifle at port arms to an area from which I supposedly could observe the enemy. When I saw the enemy I faced my leader and signaled information on the enemy. I believe that whenever a contingency plan is approved that identifies a potential enemy our senior military authority should issue the order "Scouts Out," implying that a few military intelligence "scouts" be dispatched to or near the future potential area of operations to observe, report, and plan for our next war, hoping that such scouts will be listened to and actions will be taken to avoid another case of too little too late and inadequate training. I know from experience that such an effort will be opposed strongly. I also know from experience that such can and must be done.

Brigadier General Philip B. Davidson, Jr., a West Point classmate and my successor as the Assistant Chief of Staff for Intelligence, U.S. Army, Pacific, also succeeded me in Saigon. I had recommended him to General Westmoreland as the finest officer available. I said my goodbyes and wrote the following letter to each member of the team; they were the ones who developed the organization and conducted the role of intelligence in Vietnam:

Upon my departure from this command I take pride in expressing my admiration for your unexcelled performance of duty. You have earned for military intelligence a reputation of excellence second to none. You consistently have provided timely and accurate intelligence upon which the direction and support of this war have been based. You collectively constitute the finest military intelligence team to ever support our armed forces in combat. Your past performance is magnificent history. Your future holds greater challenges and opportunities. Your capabilities are extensive. I have full confidence that you, your officers, noncommissioned officers, enlisted personnel and civilians will continue to keep intelligence out front where it belongs. It has been a great honor serving with you as a member of the First Team. Please convey my appreciation to all concerned.

APPENDIX A—J-2, MILITARY ASSISTANCE COMMAND, STAFF OFFICERS, SEPTEMBER 1965–MARCH 1967

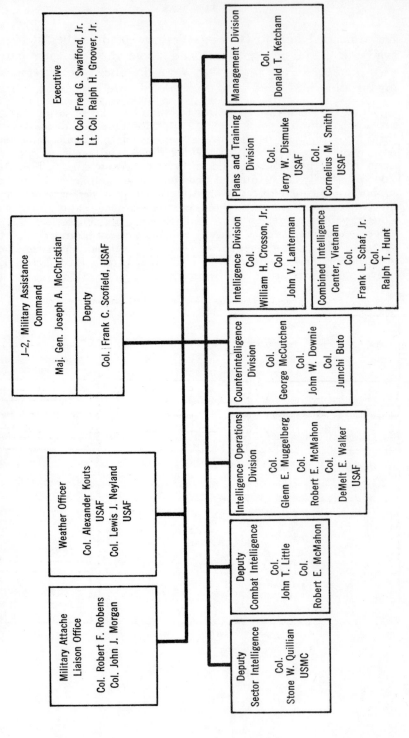

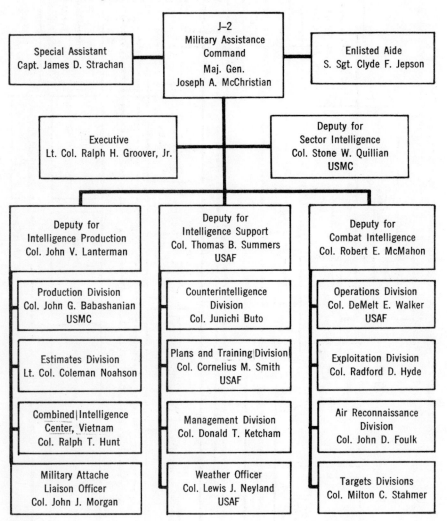

APPENDIX C—MILITARY INTELLIGENCE ORGANIZATION, 1967

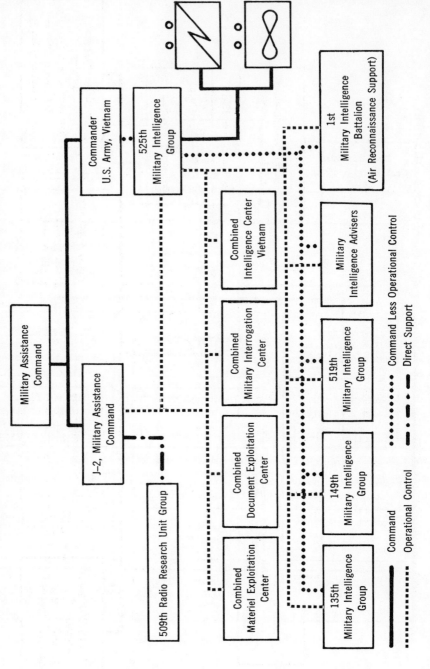

APPENDIX D—MILITARY INTELLIGENCE UNIT COMMANDERS, MID-1965—MID-1967

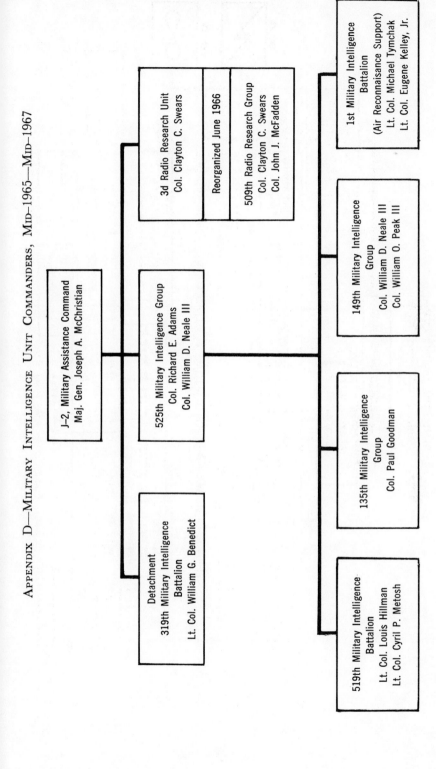

APPENDIX E—REPUBLIC OF VIETNAM ARMED FORCES MILITARY
DIVISION INTELLIGENCE DETACHMENT
(AIRBORNE–MARINE BRIGADE)

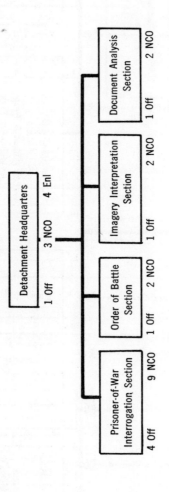

REPUBLIC OF VIETNAM ARMED FORCES MILITARY INTELLIGENCE DETACHMENT DEPLOYMENTS

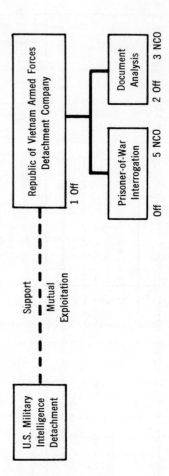

APPENDIX F—COMPATIBILITY OF J–2, JOINT GENERAL STAFF, AND J–2,
MILITARY ASSISTANCE COMMAND

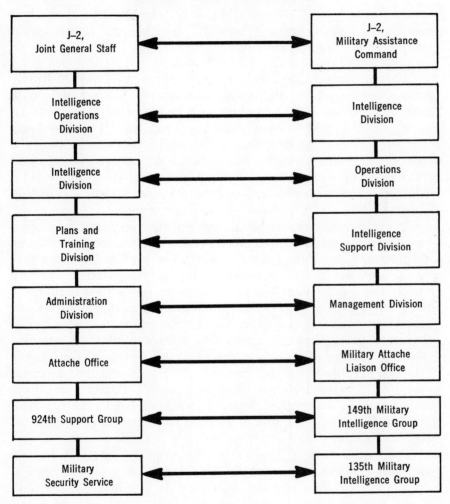

Appendix G

The following is a summary of the briefing on Viet Cong taxation presented on 8 May 1967 by J–2, Military Assistance Command, and based on a Combined Intelligence Center study completed on 1 April 1967:

This briefing is a precis of a recently updated Combined Intelligence Center study on Viet Cong taxation which was based on an analysis of interrogation reports, captured documents, agent reports, and U.S. and South Vietnamese Army files. The Viet Cong rely heavily upon the food and money which they obtain from the economy of South Vietnam. They obtain the majority of this food and money by levying taxes on the populace of the country. This briefing summarizes the various types of taxes levied by the Viet Cong and the major features of their tax system.

Several reasons apparently prompted the Viet Cong to adopt a formalized tax system. First, as the war expanded, food and money were needed in larger amounts and on a predictable basis that would allow the Viet Cong to budget for future operations. Second, a compulsory tax system had the advantage of providing them more direct control over the civilian population. Third, the Viet Cong hoped that a tax would appear to be a more legitimate technique of obtaining funds than the previously used contribution schemes, since the levying of taxes is a governmental function. Fourth, the Viet Cong realized that they needed a way to insure that revenues were not diverted into the collector's pocket. Finally, they have for many years maintained detailed census statistics covering most of South Vietnam; these statistics would facilitate the establishment of a tax system.

The tax system is directed at the national level by trained economic advisers, who comprise the finance and economic section of the Central Office of South Vietnam. At province, district, and village level, the actual operation of the tax system is carried out by the taxation and collection subsection of the echelon finance and economic section. In addition, a typical echelon finance and economic section contains several other subsections.

There has been a marked upward trend in Viet Cong tax rates as their requirements for food and revenue have grown. In addition to raising rates, the Viet Cong have attempted to increase tax revenues by enlarging the areas covered by taxes and by initiating

APPENDIX G1—FINANCE AND ECONOMIC SECTION

Accounting Subsection	Purchase and Procurement Subsection	Transportation Subsection

Taxation and Collection Subsection   Agriculture and Production Subsection

new taxes in areas already under taxation. Viet Cong revenues in 1965, of which tax collections were the chief component, were estimated at two billion piasters.

Various types of taxes are important to the enemy. At the present the Viet Cong are levying taxes on agricultural production, transportation, plantations, businesses, imports and exports, property, and income in descending order of importance. The majority of food and money derived from the tax system comes from agriculture, transportation, and marketing of agricultural products.

The rice tax, the most important of the agriculture taxes, provides the Viet Cong with their largest amounts of food and money. In fact, a directive from the Central Office of South Vietnam states that 80–90 percent of the annual Viet Cong budget is obtained through this type of taxation. Agricultural tax rates vary in different parts of the country, but on an average the Viet Cong tax 25–30 percent of the farmer's crop. In some areas, however, they have collected all of a farmer's paddy at harvest except for the amount required by his family for subsistence.

The second most important tax to the Viet Cong is the transportation tax. This tax has several advantages to the insurgents. First, it can be collected on a hit and run basis at collection points which are located on major lines of communication in areas which favor control of the road or waterway and which offer ready escape if the point is discovered. Also, since the taxes are levied on transients, the Viet Cong do not incur the discontent of a particular locale. Second, the rates can be raised quickly in order to meet current operational needs. Third, the transportation tax allows the Viet Cong to maintain a degree of control over many of the ICC's in South Vietnam. At the present time the Viet Cong are taxing literally everything that moves through their own and government-controlled areas.

Until 1966, Viet Cong taxes on plantations in South Vietnam may have been second in importance only to agricultural taxes.

These taxes have accounted for as much as half of the total Viet Cong revenues in a few provinces where there are concentrations of plantations. However, operational difficulties and the resistance of some owners to Viet Cong taxation are possibly reducing this source of funds and forcing the enemy to depend less on this form of taxation.

The tax system has two strong points. First, it is designed to draw revenue from every segment of the South Vietnamese economy. Second, the system allows for the pyramiding of taxes; that is, multiple revenues can be gained by directly or indirectly taxing a single item on each of the normal stages of production, transportation, processing, and marketing. Frequently export, import, and additional transportation taxes will be levied on an item as it passes through Viet Cong-controlled areas in route to final consumption. All of these taxes are added in arriving at the final price of the item.

APPENDIX G2—IMPACT OF VIET CONG TAXES

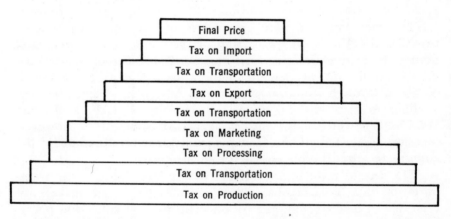

The system does contain inherent weaknesses. First, it requires that the collector and administrator be well trained if it is to work effectively. Such persons are currently in short supply for the Viet Cong. Second, increasingly heavy taxes are being levied on the populace. Discontent on the part of the people is only natural under such circumstances. Third, allied operations in an area often prevent the Viet Cong from collecting taxes.

Despite these weaknesses, the Viet Cong tax system is highly effective and supplies the enemy with substantial amounts of food, money, and control over the population.

APPENDIX H—REPUBLIC OF VIETNAM ARMED FORCES INTELLIGENCE ORGANIZATION

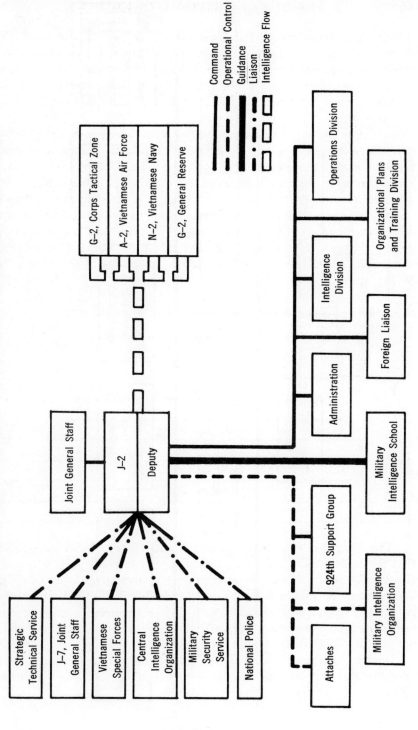

APPENDIX I—INTELLIGENCE STRUCTURE, 2D AIR DIVISION, JUNE 1965

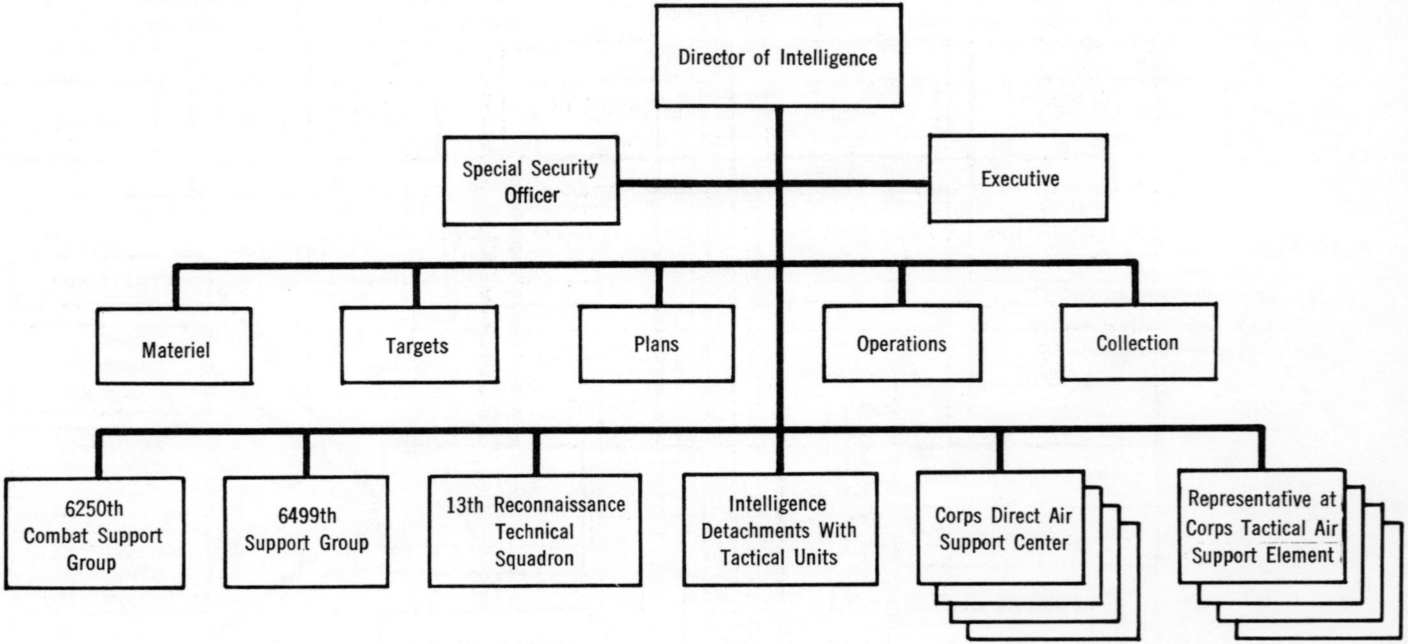

Director of Intelligence

Executive

Special Security Officer

Materiel

Targets

Plans

Operations

Collection

6250th Combat Support Group

6499th Support Group

13th Reconnaissance Technical Squadron

Intelligence Detachments With Tactical Units

Corps Direct Air Support Center

Representative at Corps Tactical Air Support Element

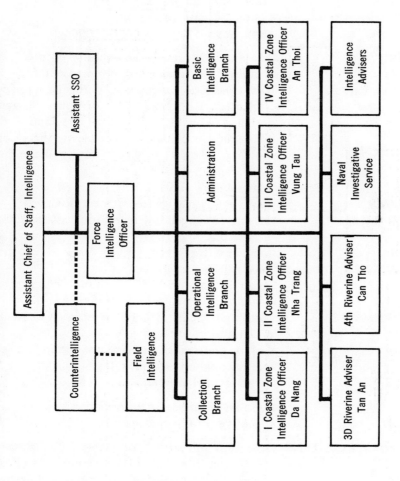

Glossary

ACofS	Assistant Chief of Staff
ADP	Automatic data processing
ARVN	Army of the Republic of Vietnam
CDEC	Combined Document Exploitation Center
CDIC	Combined Division Interrogation Center
CEDAR FALLS	Joint operation carried out by the 1st and 25th Infantry Divisions, 173d Airborne Brigade, 11th Armored Cavalry Regiment, and South Vietnamese Army units against Viet Cong Military Region IV headquarters in the Iron Triangle, 8–26 January 1967
CG	Commanding general
CICV	Combined Intelligence Center, Vietnam
CIO	Central Intelligence Organization (Republic of Vietnam)
CIS	Combined Intelligence Staff
CMD	Capital Military District
CMEC	Combined Materiel Exploitation Center
CMIC	Combined Military Interrogation Center
COMUSMACV	Commander, U.S. Military Assistance Command, Vietnam
CONCRETE	Project undertaken in 1965 to obtain imagery interpretation equipment
CTZ	Corps tactical zone
EEI	Essential elements of information
EOD	Explosive ordnance disposal
FAIRFAX/RANG DONG	Operation initiated 1 December 1966 by three U.S. and three South Vietnamese battalions with the mission of searching out and destroying the Viet Cong main force units, guerrillas, and infrastructure in Viet Cong Military Region IV
G–2	Assistant Chief of Staff for Intelligence
"Go" teams	Teams of U.S. and Vietnamese interrogators who were always ready to be dispatched from Saigon to support combat units when interrogation requirements exceeded local capabilities

IBM	International Business Machine
II	Imagery interpretation
IOD	Intelligence Operations Division
IPW	Prisoner of war interrogation
J–2	Assistant Chief of Staff for Intelligence
JUNCTION CITY	U.S.–Vietnamese operation conducted February–May 1967 in War Zone C and bordering provinces
MACV	U.S. Military Assistance Command, Vietnam
MI	Military intelligence
MIBARS	Military intelligence battalion (air reconnaissance support)
MSS	Military Security Service (Republic of Vietnam)
OB	Order of battle
PICC	Province Intelligence Coordination Committee
RVN	Republic of Vietnam
RVNAF	Republic of Vietnam Armed Forces
S–2	Intelligence officer
STARLIGHT	Operation by U.S. marines which resuted in the first major encounter between U.S. and Viet Cong forces in Vietnam, late summer 1965
TRAC	Target Research and Analysis Center
USARV	U.S. Army, Vietnam
VCI	Viet Cong infrastructure
WAYSIDE	Project undertaken by the 1st Military Intelligence Battalion (Air Reconnaissance Support) to produce annotated photomaps of U.S. installations and areas in which military operations were planned in South Vietnam

Index

☆ U.S. GOVERNMENT PRINTING OFFICE: 1975 O—532–341